FATAL
distractions

FATAL
distractions

JOYCE L. RODGERS

Charisma
HOUSE
A STRANG COMPANY

Most STRANG COMMUNICATIONS/CHARISMA HOUSE/SILOAM products are available at special quantity discounts for bulk purchase for sales promotions, premiums, fund-raising and educational needs. For details, write Strang Communications/Charisma House/Siloam, 600 Rinehart Road, Lake Mary, Florida 32746, or telephone (407) 333-0600.

FATAL DISTRACTIONS by Joyce L. Rodgers
Published by Charisma House
A Strang Company
600 Rinehart Road
Lake Mary, Florida 32746
www.charismahouse.com

Unless otherwise noted, all Scripture quotations are from the King James Version of the Bible.

Scripture quotations marked AMP are from The Amplified Bible. Old Testament copyright © 1965, 1987 by the Zondervan Corporation. The Amplified New Testament copyright © 1954, 1958, 1987 by the Lockman Foundation. Used by permission.

Scripture quotations marked NAS are from the New American Standard Bible. Copyright © 1960, 1962, 1963, 1968, 1971, 1972, 1973, 1975, 1977 by the Lockman Foundation. Used by permission. (www.Lockman.org)

Scripture quotations marked NIV are from the Holy Bible, New International Version. Copyright © 1973, 1978, 1984, International Bible Society. Used by permission.

Scripture quotations marked NKJV are from the New King James Version of the Bible. Copyright © 1979, 1980, 1982 by Thomas Nelson, Inc., publishers. Used by permission.

Cover design by
The Office of Bill Chiaravalle | www.officeofbc.com

Library of Congress Cataloging-in-Publication Data
Rodgers, Joyce L.
  Fatal distractions / Joyce L. Rodgers
      p. cm.
Includes bibliographical references.
  ISBN 1-59185-225-0 (trade paper)
  1. Christian women–Religious life. 2. Spiritual warfare. I. Title.
  BV4527.R59 2003
  248.8'43–dc22
                                        2003015425

03 04 05 06 07 — 98765432

Printed in the United States of America

Grace be unto you, and peace, from
God our Father, and from the Lord Jesus
Christ. I thank my God upon every
remembrance of you, always in every
prayer of mine for you all making request
with joy.
—Philippians 1:2–4

Dedicated to all the faithful saints
throughout the body of Christ who have
been so supportive of my ministry and me.

A special thanks to my loving mother,
"Ma Dear," my family, church family, special friends and the Primary Purpose team.

To Mrs. Winfred W. Morris and Mrs.
Michelle Calloway, thanks for the
investment.

Lastly, thank You, Jesus, for turning
areas of tragedy in my life into triumphs.
I am eternally grateful.

CONTENTS

Introduction

Fatal Distractions

T HERE IS A subtle attack taking place against women today. The Bible says that Satan was "more subtle than any other wild creature" (Gen. 3:1, RSV). He used the art of deception to lure Eve into disobedience, which eventually culminated in the Fall, ushering sin and death into the world. In other words, Satan provided the first "fatal distraction," and Eve, the mother of all mankind, fell right into his trap.

Fatal distractions are still obstacles that women face today. In the Book of Ephesians, Paul warned us to put on the whole armor of God that we might be able to stand against the "wiles" of the devil (Eph. 6:11). The word *wiles* means "a trick or stratagem intended to ensnare or deceive; trickery; guile."[1] Satan cannot attack us outright because the balance of power is in the believer's hands, but he will use every trick in the book to pull a "sneak attack" and draw us away from the things of God.

Our enemy, our "adversary the devil, as a roaring lion, walketh about, seeking whom he may devour" (1 Pet. 5:8). The Bible says that Satan is a deceiver, a liar and the father of lies. (See John 8:44.) Although he cannot defeat us, he can deceive us, and his plan of deception has unfortunately been successful against the body of Christ in general and women in particular. This plan of deception has damaged the lives of countless women who were meant to bring glory to God and victory to the body of Christ. Women everywhere are under attack as our archenemy attempts to foil our blessings, cause our spiritual gifts to be ineffective, trivialize our anointing and nullify the power working through us to deliver God's Word to hurting people.

Timing is critical in this day and age. There is a new urgency God is pressing on us to take His gospel to the world. Technology has made transmission of the gospel easy. In certain parts of the world, like the United States, you can simply turn on your television, go to your nearest Christian bookstore or find a church on virtually any street corner where you can hear the gospel. In these days, women are learning more, have more opportunities for ministry and have more authentic "power" in the kingdom of God to make significant contributions. Yet, women today have more issues of oppression: financially, physically, emotionally, spiritually and socially.

> **Women need a fresh touch from God and a new attitude of determination that God's plan will not be thwarted in their lives.**

Women both inside the church and outside the church community struggle with substance abuse and addictions—from alcohol to compulsive eating, and even to prescription drugs. Women everywhere suffer from illnesses brought on by stress and tension. Women's health-related issues rank at the top of the list of leading causes of death in America.[2] Women especially need to be healed, revived, restored, renewed and regenerated. Women need a fresh touch from God and a new attitude of determination that God's plan will not be thwarted in their lives. My prayer is that this book will bring new insight into the nature and purpose of the enemy's strategy to target women for destruction so that we can stand strongly against his attack and be victorious in the name of Christ.

CHAPTER 1

One Minute Before Midnight

SATAN HAS ALWAYS been a subtle deceiver, but now in these last days he has renewed his assault. Even as we as women move to higher levels in our spiritual walk, there are new challenges to be faced. Reaching new levels in God does not come easily. It does not come without a price tag. It does not come without a struggle. As we go higher and higher in God, Satan will mount strategic attacks to bring us down. Each level of our upward progression will be marked by another attempt to pull us off course. Have you ever heard the phrase "new devils for new levels"? As we go higher in the things of God—deeper into His Word, closer to His will and nearer to His heart—Satan's strategy gets stepped up, too.

The enemy is specific. He is focus-driven. He is obsessed with achieving his objective. He is relentless. He is ruthless, and he will go to any length to achieve his goal. He is cruel in his pursuit.

Satan's overall objective is to pull us away from the "God-plan" that has been laid out for each of our lives: the purpose for which and to which we have been called "before the foundation of the world" (Eph. 1:4).

THE CRITICAL WAITING PERIOD

I see this "God-plan" for our lives as a clear road map that God has laid out for each of us. Although the plan is designed specifically for each one, the road signs are the same for all: clearly marked speed signs and warnings of hazardous conditions to help us as we journey to the place of the fulfillment of God's purpose in our lives.

There is a critical period of time between the pronouncement of God's blessing on our lives and the manifestation of that blessing. But in that critical time of waiting for the fulfillment of the promise, Satan's attack against us often becomes the most intense. He becomes frantic and frenzied in his activity. His purpose is to distract us from the imminent fulfillment of God's promise. If he can get our focus on the "circumstances" instead of on the "certainty" of God's Word, then even after waiting through the long night, we can miss the blessing—with just one minute to go.

Women, our critical waiting period is almost over. The time is 11:59 P.M.—one minute before midnight!

Women, our critical waiting period is almost over. The time is 11:59 P.M.—one minute before midnight!

When Paul and Silas were imprisoned for their faith, their feet were bound in stocks, and their hands were chained. They were in the "stronghold"—the inner section—of the prison. (See Acts 16:16–40.) There was no chance of escape, but at 11:59 P.M. Paul and Silas began a praise and worship service in that dungeon that began to shift the stronghold! Praise God!

The word *midnight* in its most frequently used sense means the darkest point of the night: the darkest moment possible. However, in another sense, as in this case, the term *midnight* represents the turning point in a negative situation.

The word *midnight* represented the moment of deliverance for Paul and Silas, for at midnight, the angel of the Lord shook the foundations of the prison where Paul and Silas were bound, and their chains fell off (Acts 16:26).

Midnight to the Christian with the right perspective means an imminent breakthrough. Midnight means a new beginning, for a new day officially begins at 12:00 midnight. Remember, 11:59 P.M., one minute before midnight, signifies the time between the pronouncement of the blessing and the manifestation of that blessing. But ironically, even though it is the moment that is closest to the end of our waiting period, this is the time when we are most vulnerable to fatal distractions. We are most susceptible just before the moment of blessing.

Abraham and Sarah are good examples of the "One-Minute-Before-Midnight Syndrome." God had called Abram out of the land of Ur of the Chaldees and made a sevenfold covenant with him (Gen. 12). God later reconfirmed His covenant by changing Abram's name to Abraham (Gen. 17). The word *Abraham* means "the father of many." Abraham was to be the father of many nations—God promised him a son in his old age, who was to be the child of promise.

But after many years of waiting, when the night of promise seemed very long and the chances of having a child seemed slim, Sarah became impatient and gave Hagar, her servant, to Abraham to bear him a son in her stead. Weary of waiting, Abraham and Sarah thought they would "help" God fulfill His promise, but the son produced by their impatience has caused more trouble than blessing for generations.

Can you imagine the conversation between God and Abraham when Abraham confessed what he had done? Can you hear Abraham telling God that the night of waiting for the blessing had been too long? Surely Abraham brought up the fact that it was almost midnight in his life: He was at least one hundred years old, and his wife, Sarah, was ninety-nine. But God's answer defied rational thought: "Your wife, Sarah, will bear you a son, and you will call him Isaac...But my covenant I will establish with Isaac, whom Sarah will bear to you by this time next year" (Gen. 17:19, 21, author's paraphrase).

When we look at the crises of the Middle East where the descendants of Ishmael and Isaac are at war even until today, we can see that Sarah's distraction from God's plan was a fatal distraction that has reverberated through the corridors of time for more than three thousand years, causing untold heartache and bloodshed.

Fatal Distractions

Let's look at the definitions of some key terms, as I will use them throughout this book. First, the word *fatal* means "to cause death; to bring ruin; deadly."[1] It implies the process by which death is induced.

There are many definitions of the verb *distract*, from which the word *distraction* is derived. To distract can mean "to draw or direct one's attention in different directions at the same time; to stir up or confuse with conflicting emotions or motives."[2] Most of us think of to distract in this way, but few of us realize that it can also mean "to be maddened or deranged in mind; mentally confused or troubled."[3] By putting these two words together, *fatal* and *distraction*, a terrifying truth begins to emerge: If we allow Satan to distract us, we can be drawn or turned away from our spiritual position, our preordained destination or even our purpose in God's kingdom. We can turn aside from God's vision and turn instead to another direction where we die to our purpose and our ministry is brought to ruin. Such is the fate of the victims of fatal distractions.

> A fatal distraction is anything that deters you from the growth and development of your faith.

A fatal distraction is *anything that deters you from the growth and development of your faith*. It is anything or anyone who may impede the development, growth, readiness and expectation of your faith. The enemy does not want you to grow in faith. Satan knows that if you have just a little faith, even the potency of "a grain of mustard seed," you can move a mountain (Matt. 17:20).

Just imagine what one woman could do with a seed of faith! Women are powerful incubators. We can take the "seed" of a man, and in nine months we can produce a child! Imagine what an army of warring women with the "seeds" of faith could do against the strongholds of the enemy! Satan understands this, and he doesn't want us to increase our faith, exercise our faith and walk in faith. He doesn't want us to speak faith over the dead things in our lives. He doesn't want us to believe in faith, pray in faith and talk in faith. But most of all, he doesn't want us to *live in faith*.

What does Satan do to prevent our living in faith? He sends distractions, and when we are unwise, uninformed or unaware, they can become fatal distractions.

Fatal attraction

There is a movie with almost the same name as this book, *Fatal Attraction*, which contains interesting parallels to the spiritual world. It can shed some insight on our discussion of fatal distractions.

On the surface of the plot, I saw what everyone else saw: an otherwise "good" family man, Dan Gallagher, who had what he thought was a casual, consensual fling with an equally sophisticated woman, Alex Forrest. At the time, the woman was sparkling, provocative and compelling in her personality, so the man threw caution to the wind and indulged in a weekend of forbidden passion. In his mind, his weekend "fling" was just that: a fling. And while he felt somewhat guilty about his infidelity, his plan was to put it behind him. He reasoned that two responsible, consenting adults could be practical and mature about what took place, recognize and understand that what they enjoyed was only temporary, and just walk away—and he believed that the woman would look at it in the same manner.

To his dismay, he discovered that once the weekend was over, not only did the woman view their affair as the beginning of a "relationship," but also that walking away would not be as simple and easy as he had imagined. The woman began to intrude into his life with increasingly irrational obsession.

As the movie progressed, I became more and more uneasy as I saw the tremendous parallels to what goes on in the spiritual realm of our lives. The enemy attacks with the purpose of distracting us from our spiritual destiny. Remember, this man's tragedy began as a casual encounter. His life was full and content. He clearly loved his wife and doted on his child. There were no visible issues that should have driven him into the arms of another woman. He was secure and prosperous in his life, but he was distracted by something (in this case, a woman), and he fell into the trap. He could not have predicted the outcome of that encounter. Rather, the distraction was attractive—it came in a nice package that gave no hint of the unbalanced personality deep inside.

So it is in our lives with our own fatal distractions. It is usually not until we are fully engaged that their destructive natures become apparent. Ultimately, the fatal attraction the woman had to the man in the movie became fatal—not to him, but to her. The fatal distractions we allow into our own lives will fester into death: the death of our anointing; the death of our gifts and callings; and eventually, if we are not wise

> **The enemy attacks with the purpose of distracting us from our spiritual destiny.**

and apply the remedy, the death of our God-ordained purpose.

As Dan tried repeatedly to put Alex off, pay her off, change phone numbers and even move to another part of the state, she doggedly pursued him and his family and proclaimed her credo in the most famous line of the movie: "I will not be ignored!" In other words, she would intrude into his life so much that he would have to deal with her. She would threaten everything he loved until he saw how powerful she was in his life, and he would have to give her what she wanted if he hoped to survive.

Can you see how Satan, the enemy of our souls, seeks to bring the same level of distraction into *our* lives? The distraction usually begins as something small, perhaps a character fault that in itself is not necessarily unattractive or destructive. But as time progresses, it gains more power over you until what had once seemed small begins to take your mind off the plan, purpose and power of God. Your relationship to God and your faith in Him are weakened, and by the time the process is complete, it has become a fatal distraction in your life.

James 1:15 says, "When lust hath conceived, it bringeth forth sin [a distraction]: and sin, when it is finished, bringeth forth death [a fatal distraction]." Jesus stated:

> The cares and anxieties of the world and distractions of the age, and the pleasure and delight and false glamour and deceitfulness of riches, and the craving and passionate desire for other things creep in and choke and suffocate the Word, and it becomes fruitless.
>
> —MARK 4:19, AMP

The Amplified Version is so clear in this verse because it speaks of the things that come in and distract from the Word of God. It is not just enough to receive the Word; you must also take the time and effort necessary to ensure that the Word becomes productive and fruitful in you—and not just fruitful in you, but also fruitful in the people in your life. The Word must be so fruitful in you that it inspires you to do the will of God according to the plan of God.

THE *RHEMA* WORD OF GOD

Now, the enemy does not want the Word to be manifested in your life. He does not want the living Word, the *rhema* word, to take root, blossom and bring forth fruit. Moreover, he's not concerned with just the *logos*. The *logos* is the whole book, the entire Bible—from Genesis to Revelation—as it was personified in the person of Jesus Christ. However, the *rhema* is the specific word of God to you, pulled out from all the others and designed like a bullet to target you in your particular situation and station of life. The *rhema* word energizes and infuses your whole person and being, and it gives you the charge and drive that enable you to take hold of and secure the promises of God for your life.

Jeremiah spoke of the *rhema* word of God when he said, "'I know the plans I have for you,' declares the LORD, 'plans to prosper you and not to harm you, plans to give you hope and a future'" (Jer. 29:11, NIV). God has already determined your outcome, and it's good! But it cannot come to pass if you become fatally distracted.

Fatal Distractions

Satan's strategy is to steal, kill and destroy the Word planted in you—not necessarily to kill you outright, but to kill your effectiveness in ministry, kill your productivity, kill the seed within you. The fatal distraction is designed to attack your spiritual growth. The word that Satan wants to destroy is that word that is of paramount importance—to you, your ministry and ultimately to the entire body of Christ.

> The *rhema* word gives you the charge and drive that enable you to take hold of and secure the promises of God for your life.

NOT ALL DISTRACTIONS ARE FATAL!

Remember, not all distractions are fatal. As women, when we are going through such times, we may think that we're going to die—we may even *want* to die—but not every distraction will bring *spiritual* death. In the first section of this book, we will consider various *external* distractions that are not usually fatal, primarily because they are based on outside situations in our lives—problems not stemming from inside ourselves. In the second section, however, we will examine in detail eight *internal* distractions that frequently become fatal to our spiritual lives. But we will also discover their remedies, so that we can be free at last to move in the power and anointing God has for us.

I believe that God has provided answers to women everywhere who are seeking to come through their struggles successfully. My prayer is that through the words in this book, the body of Christ everywhere will be strengthened through the empowerment of women in ministry.

Women, it is time to break free of our distractions and refocus our minds and spirits onto the heart, gifts and ministry that God has designed and intends for us. Victory and triumph lie just ahead in these few pages, woman of God. Read on!

SECTION 1

NONFATAL DISTRACTIONS

CHAPTER 2

Dysfunctional Family Patterns: The Heritage of Leah

THE STORY IS one of the most powerful stories of the Bible. It contains all the drama of a modern soap opera, but unfortunately with the ring of authentic truth to which so many women can relate. It is a story of betrayal, frustration, sibling rivalry and family dysfunction that rivals any modern courtroom drama. It is the compelling love story of Rachel and Jacob, but it is also the somewhat pathetic story of the hopeless love of Leah for Jacob. However, in the end, it is also a story filled with hope and the faithfulness of God.

While family life issues might be distractions, they do not have to be *fatal* distractions. But the truth is that so often a woman's self-esteem is dependent upon the affirmation of the man with whom she is sharing a relationship, especially when that man is her husband and she is beginning a family of her own.

Leah's story, like so many of our own, began a generation earlier with her parents' generation. Genesis 29 tells us that Leah was the older daughter of Laban, and that she had a younger sister named Rachel.

Laban had become a wealthy landowner in Haran. His sister—and consequently, his daughters' aunt—Rebekah had married Isaac, the son of Abraham, and it had been prophesied that she would carry two warring nations in her womb. The twins, Esau and Jacob, were born just as the prophecy had predicted, with Jacob following Esau but with his hand grasping his older brother's heel. (See Genesis 25:26.) Jacob, although he was the younger son, was favored by Rebekah, his mother, while the older son, Esau, was favored by their father, Isaac. A situation already ripe for sibling rivalry was intensified by the behavior of the parents. Rebekah encouraged Jacob's natural tendencies to be sneaky, crafty, manipulative and cunning, to the point that Jacob ultimately cheated Esau out of his rightful birthright. It seemed for a time that Jacob had won the "war," but everything he had, he had obtained by trickery.

> **Often a woman's self-esteem is dependent upon the affirmation of the man with whom she is sharing a relationship.**

Esau wanted revenge for what he had lost—he was justifiably murderous with rage, to the point that Jacob's very life was in danger. So Rebekah sent Jacob, her favorite son, to live with her brother, his uncle Laban, until the hostility between the two brothers faded. (It should be noted that more than twenty years passed before the brothers were reunited! Some family issues can be long-term distractions, although not necessarily fatal ones.)

Into this tense family situation, Leah and her sister, Rachel, make their appearance in the story. Jacob came to live at their father's house, and the cycle of sibling rivalry began again—this time among women.

THE PATTERN CONTINUES . . .

The description that the Bible gives of these two young ladies reflects the reality that so many women face even today. As beautiful and alluring as Rachel was, Leah was her opposite:

> Leah's eyes were weak, but Rachel was beautiful of form and face. Now Jacob loved Rachel...
>
> —GENESIS 29:17–18, NAS

This situation rings true as a major distraction for women in all times and cultures, but especially in our modern society. Every woman in America has body-image issues. One need only witness the multibillion-dollar cosmetic and cosmetic surgery industries to prove this. Women today are adding, subtracting, enhancing, changing and tinting everything from their hair color to their facial and body structure. Unfortunately, these options were not available in Old Testament times, and Leah was destined to live in her younger sister's shadow. The Bible says that Rachel was "well favoured," a term that means she was vibrantly beautiful, while Leah was "tender eyed" (Gen. 29:17). This could mean a number of different problems, even that she could have been cross-eyed, but it is enough to say that Leah was not nearly as attractive as her sister!

Leah's job was to take care of the house, and such activity kept her indoors, but Rachel tended the sheep. Rachel was outdoors with the men, outdoors in the sunshine, most likely tanned and beautiful, at ease with the shepherds. And she was the first to meet the new cousin,

Jacob, at the well. An instant chemistry sparked between the two of them, and Jacob was smitten—he proposed shortly thereafter. Jacob's uncle, Laban, accepted his proposal, but a plot was underway. Laban's plan was to secretly marry off the older sister first—to Jacob! He gave one condition to his acceptance of the proposal: Jacob must work seven years of free labor to "purchase" his wife (whom he presumed would be Rachel).

During the wedding ceremony, a party that lasted for several days and featured a great deal of wine, Leah was substituted for her sister in the bridal chamber. The resulting deception was not discovered by Jacob until the following morning—but it was too late. Even as Jacob raged at his new father-in-law about the trick, he knew it was too late. But Jacob wasn't the one who was harmed the most in the exchange: Both husband and father beat down Leah's self-esteem as she heard Jacob declare that he did not love her but loved her sister, Rachel, instead. She heard her father bargain away her life as he promised Jacob that he could wed Rachel for another seven years of labor. So after a brief "honeymoon" with an unwilling husband, Leah was to share him with the love of his life—her own sister, her oldest and deepest rival.

If ever there was a potentially fatal distraction in Leah's life, this situation should have been it! Under these circumstances, Leah might have become emotionally unstable, depressed or even suicidal. Women in our day have cracked under lesser pressures than Leah faced. For years she lingered in a relationship that threatened to destroy her both emotionally and spiritually and detour her permanently from her God-ordained path.

In fact, the names that Leah gave her children during this incredibly difficult time in her life show the mental turmoil and emotional heartbreak she was experiencing. Scripture records that because God "saw that Leah was hated, he opened her womb: but Rachel was barren" (Gen. 29:31). When her first son was born, Leah named him *Reuben*, which means, "Behold, a son."[1] Every time Jacob called his son's name, he would be made to remember that Leah had done what every man wanted: She had given him a firstborn son.

Leah stopped looking to find her life in another person and instead began to recognize that her life, joy, fulfillment and purpose all came from walking the path of destiny that God had ordained for her.

Nevertheless, the distraction in Leah's life continued. Nothing changed in her relationship with her husband. The Bible says that God again took pity on Leah and opened her womb a second time. She named her second son *Simeon*, which means, "God hears," a sign that she still had faith that God could turn her situation around.[2] Surely God had heard her sorrow and prayers for her marriage to be healed. Surely God had seen her tears of rejection and heartbreak. But there was still no change. Wasn't He listening?

A third son was born. This one Leah named *Levi*, a name that means "joined."[3] Leah's desire for a loving husband had become desperate. At this point she was so starved for love and attention that she craved simple companionship—and she began to seek fulfillment of this craving in her children. Her distraction was on the brink of becoming a *fatal distraction.*

Leah was losing sight of her God-given purpose. She was allowing her bad marriage and her emotional needs to blind her to the *rhema*, the life-giving word that was meant to be her destiny.

Fortunately, Leah was able to shift her focus. She took her eyes off her circumstances and put her eyes—weak as they were—on God. She stopped looking to find her life in another person and instead began to recognize that her life, joy, fulfillment and purpose all came from walking the path of destiny that God had ordained for her.

How do we know that this change took place? When Leah's fourth son was born, she demonstrated that her "love line" was now directed vertically toward God instead of horizontally to Jacob. She named this son *Judah,* which means "praise."[4] Moreover, Scripture says that she "left bearing" (Gen. 29:35). While this literally means that she ceased to have any more children, in a metaphorical sense it could mean that she stopped living for Jacob and began living for God. In other words, she derailed the distraction before it had a chance to become fatal to her future. She changed her focus from an earthly one to a heavenly one, and God put her back on course to fulfill her rightful destiny.

Even the heartbreak of broken relationships, something that millions of women in this country can relate to, does not have to become a fatal distraction in your life! Once Leah understood the power of praise in her life, her "tender eyes" saw more clearly than they had ever seen before.

The Rest of the Story . . .

However, that's not the end of the story. Generations later, the true blessing of Leah's heritage was birthed: When the nation of Israel was born and the inheritances of the tribes were given, Leah's sons were to play a prominent role. The lineage of Levi became the tribe of the priesthood: Every priest in Jewish history was to come out of the tribe of Levi, Leah's son, including Moses and Aaron. And every legitimate king after the reign of Saul came out of Judah, Leah's son. King David came out of the tribe of Judah, Leah's son. King Solomon came out of the tribe of Judah, Leah's son. Jesus, our Savior, the Lion of the tribe of Judah, came from the lineage of Judah, Leah's son.

There is a purpose. God has a plan. If Satan had been able to fatally distract Leah, God's ultimate plan would still have been fulfilled, but the whole blessing of Judah would have been lost. Instead, Judah's praises rang out through the centuries. Jehoshaphat's great victory was won by sending the praises of Judah, the descendants of Leah, first.

> **Don't let the distraction of family heartbreak become a fatal distraction.**

This word is to encourage you—wherever you are in your life—as you struggle with family issues. Don't let the distraction of family heartbreak become a fatal distraction. Remember the model of Leah. She stayed on track and reached the promised end that God had ordained for her.

CHAPTER 3

Job Concerns: The "Martha Syndrome"

Job Concerns: The "Martha Syndrome"

ALL DISTRACTIONS FROM the plan of God—whether fatal or nonfatal—come from the enemy of mankind, who has been at war with humanity since their creation in the Garden of Eden. Even before that time, Satan had attempted to usurp the worship that belongs only to God, and along with his crew of rebel angels, he waged war in heaven, eventually to be cast down to the earth. Ever since, his presence in the earth has been as the archenemy of mankind, his sole purpose being to distract mankind from its purpose. He lured Eve, the mother of us all, with the first fatal distraction, and she in turn distracted Adam from his God-ordained path. This cataclysmic event, the Fall of man, brought curses and punishments for both Adam and Eve, and to each of us as their descendants. Sin and death had entered the world.

God called each of the participants in the rebellion in Eden into account. The Spirit of God, moving through the garden in the cool of the evening, called out, "Adam, where art thou?" (Gen. 3:9). The scope of the tragedy can be seen when Adam, who had once enjoyed an intimate spiritual fellowship with God, now hid in terror from the wrath and judgment of a holy God. His answer to God's simple question reveals his newfound guilt: "I was hiding because of my nakedness." (See Genesis 3:10.) When God questioned Adam as to how he knew he had "no covering," Adam's reply was to immediately shift direct blame to the woman and indirect blame to God Himself by saying, "The woman whom You gave me—she caused me to eat!" (See Genesis 3:12.)

There are two important things to note in all of this. The first is that although Adam had made a covering of leaves for himself and Eve, God saw that as an inadequate covering for their sin. God Himself slew an animal and used its skin as a covering for man's sin: "Unto Adam also and to his wife did the Lord God make coats of skins, and clothed them" (Gen. 3:21). This first shedding of blood to cover sin foreshadowed the magnificent sacrifice of Jesus who would also be slain, but His blood would be the covering for the sins of all of mankind.

> **All distractions from the plan of God—whether fatal or nonfatal—come from the enemy of mankind.**

Our second point is that the penalties given by God to each of the participants established consequences for all succeeding generations of mankind. First, the ease of life that Adam and Eve had previously known was lost. From that time forward, Adam would have to earn his food by hard labor—by the "sweat of his brow" (v. 19, NIV). No longer would the garden yield its bountiful harvest to him effortlessly. Now even the ground was cursed for his sake. Eve, on the other hand, would be greatly increased in her sorrow and in her conception, and she would bear her children in pain (v. 16). Finally, the serpent would be forced to crawl on its belly, but more importantly, enmity was established between the seed of the woman and the serpent, foreshadowing the struggle between Jesus and Satan at Calvary where Christ would emerge the victor with all power in His hands.

Despite these serious consequences handed down by God, perhaps the most devastating consequence of all was the disruption of God's order for mankind, especially where the family was concerned. Roles for men and women that had been established by God for the good of all became blurred and over time have virtually disappeared. In the culture in which I was raised, traditionally, men were to be the breadwinners, and women were to be the homemakers. However, the fact is that, at least in twenty-first-century America, that set of roles frequently does not apply. Unfortunately, social factors being what they are, the breakdown of the traditional roles of men and women has meant that millions of women are not just the homemakers, but they are the breadwinners as well.

In millions of homes, the only parent is a single female parent who labors outside as well as inside the home. But even in the homes and families in which there are two parents, large numbers of women work outside the home. These women are "multitasking" themselves to the limit! While most women have a God-given ability to do numerous tasks at the same time, most women in America can relate to having too much to do and too little time, energy or ability to get it all done. The result is that the next day, the tasks left over from the day before are still there to be done—in addition to the new day's list. And every day, the list of "undone chores" and "to-do tasks" gets higher and higher.

The stress associated with never-ending demands on a woman's time, energy, body and spirit means that eventually health issues will occur. Women in twenty-first-century America are facing more stress-related physical ailments and psychological burnout than ever before. Numerous illnesses are directly related to the stress of women's lifestyles and the multiple roles they must fulfill.[1] Women today suffer from what I call the "Martha Syndrome," which, while it is a distraction, does not have to necessarily become a fatal one.

THE MARTHA SYNDROME

The story of Lazarus and his two sisters, Mary and Martha, all close friends of Jesus, is a familiar one to most of us. Their home was one where Jesus and His disciples frequently came to visit during their years of ministry. They lived in Bethany, a little town that was near Jerusalem, yet far enough away from the hustle and bustle of the big city to be a peaceful respite when Jesus needed to rest.

Hospitality was a trademark of the society in Palestine in that day, and the role of the women of the house was clearly defined: Mary and Martha were the ones who were responsible for serving and attending to the guests in their home. But this was not a task to be taken lightly. In fact, hospitality was so significant in biblical times that one of the qualifications for becoming a minister, according to Paul, was that one must be "given to hospitality" (1 Tim. 3:2).

The rules for the treatment of guests were very specific. Throughout the history of many different cultures, guests in the home of a powerful lord could claim protection, sanctuary from pursuers, food or shelter through the right of hospitality. Moreover, the servants and companions of the traveler and guests also had a claim on the household to share whatever provisions were available.

When all of these cultural—and biblical—factors are considered, it would not be hard to come to the conclusion that Martha was correct to be the "busy" sister, hurrying about to see that all of the necessary preparations were on track. I can almost picture Martha, early in the morning, knowing that Jesus was coming, working herself into a frenzy getting the fresh bread baked, the meat dressed for the roasting, fresh vegetables prepared, wine, fresh fruit

> **While many are quick to judge Martha for her "unwise priorities," it should be noted that her priorities were, in fact, necessary.**

and figs, raisins and dates all arranged on festive platters and in jugs. She would have the foot basins ready to wash the dusty feet of the travelers upon their arrival, as the custom of the day required. She would have made sure there were enough clean straw pallets for each of Jesus' twelve companions who had traveled with Him to rest for the night, and that all was ready for the comfort and nourishment of this large crew of hungry men for a visit of several days.

When Jesus and His disciples finally arrived, Martha was still "encumbered" about many things. But while many are quick to judge Martha for her "unwise priorities," it should be noted that her priorities were, in fact, necessary. They were things that were essential to keep a well-ordered household running smoothly.

Don't women face the same dilemma today? The kids need to get to school. Lunches need to be packed. Projects have to be completed for the Science Fair. Johnny needs to get to his music lessons, and Janie needs to get to soccer practice. There is a committee meeting for the PTA, Boy Scouts and Girls Scouts, but they are all on the same night as choir rehearsal or Bible study.

Each day the modern-day Martha begins a little further behind, and soon her "quiet time" with the Lord is crowded out.

The evaluations for the new employees need to be written. An elderly parent who may be recovering from a stroke needs to be checked on daily. And this does not even include the "normal" chores that have to be done each day to maintain an active family, even with everyone pitching in, let alone the needed time to be a wife and a person in your own right.

So why did Jesus rebuke Martha? Herein lies the trap: Women are so easily "encumbered" about many things, most of which are necessary! Taking care of a household is necessary. Caring for a husband and children is necessary. And yes, even jobs outside the home are sometimes necessary. Very few households can operate successfully with only one income in today's economy. Sadly, the reality in America today is that most women need to work outside the home; therefore, women have to be multitasked. They have to be almost "Superwomen" to meet all of the many necessary demands on their lives.

But as the modern-day Martha falls into bed at the end of the day, she has trouble falling asleep because her mind is already racing over the next day's to-do list, trying to plan how to work "double-time" because of what had to be missed from that day. Each day she begins a little further behind, and soon her "quiet time" with the Lord—the time to meditate on the Word, the time to fellowship with God in prayer, the time to wake up early in the morning to check God's schedule and see what He would have her do that day—is crowded out. Instead of following His pace for her life, she becomes distracted by all that she "has" to do.

The good news is that this does not have to become a fatal distraction! Martha kept returning to the room where Jesus was seated as He shared His wisdom and teaching with His disciples. Mary, Martha's sister, was sitting quietly at Jesus' feet, drinking in the Master's parables, words and instructions. She felt the comfort of His presence in an intimate setting where she could ask questions just as the disciples asked and hear Jesus' answers firsthand.

Mary realized that this was an opportunity not to be missed! Consider what that must have been like—how precious His words must have been, how much insight Mary gained by hearing Jesus' direct instructions. And think how clearly Martha's destiny could have been shown to her, but instead, Martha was encumbered by "busy-ness," not God's "business"!

Satan uses this subtle distraction on women in particular with great success. And the trap is that all of the things that Martha did were necessary tasks! But while her chores made life more comfortable for everyone in the house, by being so burdened with the tasks *themselves*, Martha had lost sight of the *purpose* of the tasks: to serve her Lord, to minister to Jesus' needs, to give the Master what He needed and what He wanted!

How many women in churches are so busy with *church work*, that they lose sight of the *work of the church*? Jesus' rebuke to Martha holds true for every overextended woman today:

> "Martha, Martha," the Lord answered, "you are worried and upset about many things, but only one thing is needed. Mary has chosen what is better, and it will not be taken away from her."
>
> —Luke 10:41, NIV

NECESSARY, BUT NOT A DISTRACTION

Work and multiple responsibilities can become a distraction of the enemy to keep you from focusing on the right priorities. In essence, Jesus told Martha, "Work is good, but keep it in the proper perspective." It should never replace "what is better"—the balance, the love for her Savior—that Mary had chosen.

Woman of God, do the necessary things, but don't become encumbered by them. Don't become a workaholic who leaves her relationship with the Master on the "things-to-do-tomorrow list."

Instead, "seek ye first the kingdom of God, and his righteousness; and all these things shall be added unto you" (Matt. 6:33). In other words, you can have it all as long as your priorities are straight. Feed your soul first. Feed your inner man first. Feed your relationship with God first. Talk to God first about the order of your day. Let Him order your steps and set your schedule. Your days will be more profitable to Him as well as yourself. You don't have to let your distraction of "busy-ness" become the fatal distraction of missing God's "business" for your life.

CHAPTER 4

Health Issues: The Woman With the Issue of Blood

NOTHING AFFECTS US like our health. Even though we are spiritual beings, we live in frail human bodies. All of our spiritual gifts, all of our anointing and all of the potential for ministry we have been given by God is housed in earthen vessels—our flesh. We are subject to the same processes of aging and disease as anyone else. In fact, health-related issues are some of the most challenging distractions we will face on this earth, and on more than just a spiritual level, they can literally become fatal distractions.

Among Christians, however, there is an additional psychological burden to face: the idea—however unrealistic it might be—that we should be "above" certain human frailties. We are expected to be great prayer warriors who have unhindered access to the throne of God. The gifts of supernatural healing flow through our hands for others. We may even have the gift of miracles that manifests everywhere else but in our own bodies.

THE DISTRACTION OF PHYSICAL SICKNESS

What happens, then, when we are the ones who are sick and afflicted? What has gone wrong? In the privacy of our

41

own thoughts, in the secret places in our own spirits, we may wonder what God is doing in our lives. At that point, our health has become a distraction in our spiritual walk.

Moreover, Satan reserves his most intense attacks—especially in the area of sickness and disease—for the "strongest" of the anointed ones. A fitting example of this is demonstrated in the Old Testament Book of Job.

> Health-related issues are some of the most challenging distractions we will face on this earth.

According to the Bible, Satan went into God's presence to challenge Him to a contest regarding Job's faithfulness and spiritual integrity. It was Satan's hypothesis that Job was not serving God out of a true heart, but instead he served God because of the multiple blessings he had received. After stripping Job bit by bit of his material goods, prestige, wealth and even his family, Satan found that Job still maintained his integrity before the Lord. Finally Satan decided to pull out what he thought was his heaviest artillery: Job's physical health. He said:

> All that a man has he will give for his life. But put forth thy hand now, and touch his bone and his flesh, and he will curse thee to thy face.
> —Job 2:4–5, RSV

Although this was a terrible boast for Satan to make, it did demonstrate his understanding of human nature. Fortunately, in Job's case, he was able to resist Satan's temptation to curse God; instead, he stood strong in his faith. But Satan hasn't given up; he continues to use this distraction to this day, often successfully.

The Holy Spirit has inspired me to warn the women in God's church not to let the enemy pull us away from God with the distraction of health problems. Although illness can be painful, heartbreaking and often incomprehensible, it doesn't have to be spiritually fatal to us as well.

I am so glad that God loves women! I am so glad that He values us enough to put our stories in the Bible as well. And God is so concerned with the health concerns of women that He put our story, even a gender-specific one, in the Scriptures just for us: the account of the woman with the issue of blood.

The stories of the Bible are perfect examples for us to look at and use as a pattern for our lives. They are especially encouraging when we can truly identify with them. The story of the woman with the issue of blood could only be a woman's story. It is one of the most powerful miracles that Jesus ever performed, but it also shows us how physical sickness can become a near-fatal distraction in our lives.

Although we don't know what the woman's health issue was specifically, we can infer that it was a chronic, debilitating, apparently incurable—not to mention embarrassing—illness that was wasting her life away. Already it had robbed her of so many things: her health, her finances, her relationships, her social status and even her religious participation. And it was long lived. For more than twelve years she had faced the isolation, the discomfort and the loneliness brought on by her chronic condition. What a terrible distraction to face.

According to the Mosaic Law, the woman's condition made her ceremonially unclean; she would have been barred from participation in worship with her congregation. Shut off from fellow believers, she might have become disillusioned with those "saints" who rejected her. (How like many of our churches today!)

The woman had done all that was required of her by her society. No doubt she had done what the Law of Moses required of her. She had exhausted the limits of medical science, for the Bible says she spent all of her financial resources on doctors and their prescriptions, but despite all of their efforts, her condition got steadily worse.

All of these problems could have become a fatal distraction for this woman—both spiritually and physically. Nevertheless, the Bible says that "faith cometh by hearing" (Rom. 10:17). Remember, my sisters, we must not get so distracted by the symptoms we are feeling in our bodies that we miss the more important symptoms in our spirits! God may be speaking to us even in our sickness, but we may not be hearing Him through our pain.

That is the real power that physical sickness can have as a distraction. Human nature is such that we tend to focus on our own discomfort and the apparent "unfairness" of God in allowing such a thing to happen to us—rather than concentrate on His faithfulness.

NO LONGER AN ISSUE

No doubt even in her isolated state, the woman with the issue of blood could *hear* the multitudes shouting on the road that day. No doubt she had *heard* that the miracle-working Rabbi was passing by on His way to the house of

Jairus, the ruler of the synagogue. She *heard* that His power had healed all manner of illnesses, even leprosy, and this caused her *faith* to leap into action. She would not allow her illness to be a distraction any longer!

No doubt the woman knew she might not get close to Jesus. She could have given up and thought she was too weak from blood loss to push her way through the crowd for a face-to-face consultation with the Master. She likely realized that her own Jewish tradition would prevent her from touching Him, a Rabbi, due to the fact that she was ceremonially unclean. Nevertheless, she purposed in her heart that if she could just touch the hem of His garment—the borders of His clothes—she would be made whole. (See Matthew 9:20–21.)

> No health problem, no physical condition should cause us to lose sight of the path of destiny that God has mapped out for us.

The message to women today is clear: No health problem, no physical condition should cause us to lose sight of the path of destiny that God has mapped out for us. Like the obstacles that faced the woman with the issue of blood, women's health issues can easily become distractions: often powerful, painful, protracted, even paralyzing problems. But they do not have to become fatal distractions! When the woman with the "issue" of blood got close enough to really touch Jesus, it just wasn't an "issue" any longer.

CHAPTER 5

The Ticking Biological Clock: Hannah's Prayer of Relinquishment

GETTING MARRIED AND having children is the number-one dream of most women—and for good reason: We were created with a heart for the family, and children are a reward from God, as we read in Psalm 127:3:

> Lo, children are an heritage of the LORD: and
> the fruit of the womb is his reward.

But for the single woman who has not yet found her soul mate, or for the married woman who, for whatever reason, has not been able to have a child, the ticking of the biological clock can grow so loud at times that it can drown out any voice of reason or sanity. Our arms ache for the husband we long to love, for the children we hope to bear, but if we are not careful, these desires can run rampant and become a fatal distraction in our lives.

UNHAPPILY SINGLE

I first want to address the woman who is still waiting to find that "special someone" with whom to spend the rest of her life. You know who you are! Your "biological clock" is ticking, and your despair is deepening—not only because you are afraid of never experiencing the joy of marriage, but also because it seems you will also be denied the experience of bearing a child.

The people around you don't usually help the situation. Well-wishers tell you, "Honey, this is your year—your blessing is on the way!" (Never mind that they told you that five years ago, and your "blessing" isn't here yet!) You have been prophesied to, prayed for, called out and touched and agreed with. You have been on more blind dates than you can count. The older ladies in the church have swung from pitying you to looking at you suspiciously and asking, "Baby, why is it that you never bring a man as a visitor to our services?"

> The ticking of the biological clock can grow so loud at times that it can drown out any voice of reason or sanity.

You have been in at least ten weddings, and you have the hideous bridesmaid dresses in your closet to prove it. The pressure has gotten so intense that every time a new brother sets foot in the doors of the church, you find yourself asking, "Lord, is that him?" Unfortunately, not only are you asking God that question, but also the twenty-two other single women in your church are asking Him the same thing!

Listen, I know how tough it is to be single and to wonder if you will ever find the right person. I know what singles groups in many churches are like, including those singles bowling nights and backyard barbecues! I know how difficult the holidays can be on your own and how hard it is to watch your other friends get married and have children. But if you are not careful, you can become so wrapped up in praying for and looking for a mate that you lose the focus on your life—and the destiny that God has for you. And then your "barrenness" has become not just a distraction, but a fatal one.

My word to you, my single and waiting sister, is to take heart and concentrate your attention upon the ultimate Lover of your soul, our Lord and Savior Jesus Christ. No, I don't have any words of prophecy for you; I'm not going to mislead or insult you by trying to hype you up that your soul mate is waiting for you just around the next corner— you've already been there and done that. And you're still single. What I will tell you is to love God and love yourself.

Don't permit yourself to settle for less than God's best by submitting to unsatisfactory relationships or covenants with ungodly men, all for the sake of just having a man in your life.

Don't let the ticking of your biological clock distract you either. If God is in control of your life, He has the perfect timing already planned out.

In the Old Testament, as Joshua was battling his enemies, God had already granted him a great victory, but some of the enemies were fleeing and he needed more time to complete the conquest:

> Then spake Joshua to the LORD in the day when the LORD delivered up the Amorites before the children of Israel, and he said in the sight of Israel, Sun, stand thou still upon Gibeon; and thou, Moon, in the valley of Ajalon.
> —JOSHUA 10:12

Joshua literally asked time to stand still, and it did!

> And the sun stood still, and the moon stayed, until the people had avenged themselves upon their enemies. Is not this written in the book of Jasher? So the sun stood still in the midst of heaven, and hasted not to go down about a whole day.
>
> —Joshua 10:13

Now the Bible does say that this particular miracle will never be repeated: "And there was no day like that before it or after it, that the Lord hearkened unto the voice of a man: for the Lord fought for Israel" (v. 14). But my point is that, if necessary, God has the power to make time stand still for you! In other words, don't be afraid of the time that is passing in your life, for God will give you enough time to not only *receive*, but also *enjoy* the blessings He has planned for you. He alone opens doors that no man can shut (Rev. 3:8). Trust in His ability to provide you with the spouse *and* the children you desire, but more than that, trust in His deep, abiding and unfailing love *for you.*

If God is in control of your life, He has the perfect timing already planned out.

Married, Without Children

What about the heartache of being married, but for whatever reason, you seem unable to bear a child? How can you cope with the deprivation of something so integral to your womanhood? God's Word is true when it likens barrenness to a land that is parched by drought:

There are three things that are never satisfied,
yea, four things say not, It is enough: The
grave; and the barren womb; the earth that is
not filled with water; and the fire that saith not,
It is enough.

—PROVERBS 30:15–16

God understands the pain and angst of a childless
woman—and His response toward Hannah demonstrates
how much He cares.

Hannah's story is told in the Book of First Samuel, and it
takes place at a time in which polygamy was an accepted
practice. Because a man would have several wives, it gave the
women a certain status in the family when they were able to
bear children—especially sons—for their husbands. Hannah's
husband, Elkanah, had another wife named Peninnah who
had borne him several children, but Hannah's womb was
barren. The Bible tells us that Peninnah took joy in making
Hannah's life miserable: "And her adversary [Peninnah] also
provoked her sore, for to make her fret, because the LORD
had shut up her womb" (1 Sam. 1:6). Sadly, there are some
wounds that women inflict upon each other that cut to the
bone, and this was one of them.

Many "barren" women today may not have to face
another wife in their husband's household, or even other
women with such malicious attitudes, but they can likely
relate to seeing pregnant women and mothers with children everywhere they turn. It seems that the more
someone wants to have a child of her own, the more baby
showers for others she is invited to attend!

Fortunately for Hannah, she had an understanding husband, but nothing but a child would seem to fill the void in

her heart. Well-meaning people may have told her—as many do today—"Don't worry about it, honey. God knows what's best." Or, "The world is so wicked these days; why would you even want to bring a child into it?" But the pain and longing in Hannah's heart were so great that she had become unable to eat. Elkanah even said to her, "Hannah, why are you weeping? Why don't you eat? Why are you downhearted? Don't I mean to you more than ten sons?" (1 Sam. 1:8, NIV). His well-meaning words could not fill the void in Hannah's soul. And Hannah was well on her way to allowing a fatal distraction to destroy her life.

Fortunately, Hannah reached out to God in her time of need and reorganized her priorities to align with His. As she cried out to God in the temple, out of the anguish of her soul, she made a vow that if He would give her a son, she would return the child to the Lord for life-long service in His temple. And her prayer was answered. She was blessed with a child, Samuel, whom she consecrated to the Lord, and who later became one of the Old Testament judges. God performed above and beyond what Hannah had asked in her prayer, and she went on to have five more children besides!

> We are the children of a sovereign God who does indeed love us and is faithful to give us the strength we need to go through any trial, no matter how heartbreaking or severe.

Although Hannah's story had a happy ending, there are scores of women today who are not so fortunate—they remain childless. They go through life distracted by the belief that their highest mission as a woman is going unfulfilled, their prayers for a child unanswered. Maybe they had been able to conceive, but lost their child through miscarriage. To conceive and then for whatever reason be unable to carry a child to full term is especially heartbreaking. In addition to grieving the loss of the child, a woman often experiences a sense of failure and guilt: Did she do something to cause the miscarriage? Why did the pregnancy fail? Who was that child?

Another heartache that may be experienced is that of giving birth to a stillborn child, or to a child that lives only a very short time. All of these experiences can be excruciating and can cause even the strongest woman to experience great sadness and even depression.

I have no answer for these occurrences, except to say that we are the children of a sovereign God who does indeed love us and is faithful to give us the strength we need to go through any trial, no matter how heartbreaking or severe. He tells us in Isaiah 43:1–2:

> Fear not: for I have redeemed thee, I have called thee by thy name; thou art mine. When thou passest through the waters, I will be with thee; and through the rivers, they shall not overflow thee: when thou walkest through the fire, thou shalt not be burned; neither shall the flame kindle upon thee.

There will be times in our lives when we experience trials and tribulations that are as devastating to our lives and emotions as a fire or a flood. The pain we feel during these times can burn like the hottest flame; the emotions we struggle with can make us feel as if we are indeed drowning. As one woman who lost her child said, "I felt like I was on a roller coaster, and my life was turned upside down. I was walking around, but on the inside I felt like the whole world was facing in another direction than I was."

To that, the Lord speaks to us the words of a precious promise contained in Isaiah 41:10:

> Fear thou not; for I am with thee: be not dismayed; for I am thy God: I will strengthen thee; yea, I will help thee; yea, I will uphold thee with the right hand of my righteousness.

If you are experiencing an overwhelming sense of grief at the loss of your child through miscarriage, stillbirth or even sudden infant death syndrome, pray this prayer to the God who understands your pain:

> *Father, in the name of Jesus, I come before Your throne to find grace and mercy in this time of need. Lord, You said that You would satisfy the longing soul and fill the hungry soul with goodness. You told us that the sacrifices of God are a broken heart and a contrite spirit, that a contrite spirit You would not despise. I come before You with a broken heart and a broken spirit, and I look to You to give me consolation and peace. Touch me right now, in the name of Jesus. Touch me in the deepest part of my soul, and satisfy the longing that is there. Satisfy my longing and fill my bereaved soul with Your goodness. Take away the emptiness, Lord; take away the emptiness.*
>
> *God, I come against the enemy that would seek to bring depression and a sense*

of guilt and failure into my life. I cast those imaginations down in the name of Jesus, and I speak peace, healing and wholeness of mind, body, soul and spirit into my life. Help me, Lord, in the areas I need You the most. Fill my soul with praise and thanksgiving, for You are my God, my sword and shield. You are my Rock, my High Tower and my Protector; Your banner over me is love.

Father, in the name of Jesus, give me an overwhelming sense of Your presence and Your love, and fill me with Your grace. Help those around me to speak godly words, words that will comfort me, edify me and build me up. My Father, I give You the glory and honor and praise, in Jesus' name. Amen.

Although the lack of children may loom largely over your head and obscure the other blessings in your lives, there is always hope. Notice how Hannah handled her distraction: Despite the irritating jeers of Peninnah, her loss of appetite, the river of tears she had cried and the longing of her barren womb, Hannah reached the point where she was able to cast her care upon the Lord, because deep down, she *knew* He cared for her. When you are dealing with a distraction of this nature and magnitude, you must shift your focus away from what you *lack* and place it upon what you *have* because you are a child of God.

Just as the three Hebrew boys said when they were facing the fiery furnace, we must also say, "If it be so, our God whom we serve is able to deliver us from the burning fiery furnace...But if not...we will not serve thy gods" (Dan. 3:17–18). Our attitude must be, "Whether God does or does not answer my prayer, I will yet love Him. I will yet live for Him, and I will yet celebrate my Lord and my life in Christ. I will yet praise Him, for He is the King of kings and Lord of lords. He is my Shepherd, and in Him I have no lack."

Shift the focus away from what you *lack* and place it upon what you *have* because you are a child of God.

Defeat this distraction and find peace in your spirit by zeroing in on the great love your heavenly Father has for you, His precious daughter. When you center your heart in His love, you will find rest, solace and comfort, as well as a greater understanding of the destiny that He has for your future.

CHAPTER 6

Marital Problems: The Positive Attitude of Abigail

Perhaps the greatest distraction many women will face in their lives is the heartbreak of a difficult marriage. The heart of a woman was made for relationship—God created us that way! Our sensitivity to emotional experiences predisposes us to the strong and binding ties of relationships. And the socialization of our culture causes women to focus on their relationships: their families, children, marriages, friends and significant others. Christian women are not immune to this distraction. Even though we realize that we should focus our attention on the things of the Spirit, our hearts still yearn and burn for a relationship with a loving husband. Unfortunately, our vulnerability in this area can make us a target in the spiritual realm, as Satan wars against our souls, our purpose, our anointing, our mission and our godly purpose.

The reason that relationships are so important to women is that the home, the family, was the first social institution created by God. Recall that in the Book of Genesis, God created the first man, Adam, and then He brought the woman to him. In this first relationship between human beings, God created a family, designed to reflect the attributes of God's heavenly family.

Like the heavenly family, the earthly family had divine purpose: to produce worshipers who would glorify God. God intended the family to be the building block of every other social institution on earth. Because of this, one of Satan's greatest strategies has been to disrupt the harmony of the home, for by doing so he could thwart future generations of godly worshipers and spiritual warriors who would eventually destroy his kingdom.

> **The home, the family, was the first social institution created by God.**

Satan has always sought to destroy marriages, for they are the foundation of the family, and as they are weakened, so is the whole fabric of society.

After the Fall, sin entered the world, and the perfect relationship between the first husband and wife, Adam and Eve, was disrupted by mistrust, shame and blame. These elements trickled down to the first generation of children ever born, Cain and Abel. The tragic outcome of their sibling rivalry was the first physical death of a human being—caused by murder.

Satan's successful attack on the first family in Genesis has allowed him to target every family on the face of the earth ever since. I don't have to know your life story to know that the enemy has attacked, or will soon attack, your home, your family or your marriage. His greatest scheme is to distract you by attacking those close to you. Many marriages today are plagued by financial stress, child-rearing disputes, fidelity issues, bickering among in-laws, substance abuse issues or even domestic violence.

These are tools of Satan that he uses to eat away at the foundation of the family and trap you in a fatal distraction.

But thanks be to God! He has given us His Word, and in it He has provided a role model for dealing with a difficult marriage without allowing the distraction to become a fatal one. Yes, our hearts may be hurt. Yes, our relationships may be less than we want them to be. But God shows us how to respond through the Old Testament story of Abigail and Nabal.

ABIGAIL: A POSITIVE MODEL

First Samuel 25 tells of the marriage of one woman who had every reason to lose her focus on her God-given destiny by the circumstances of a bad marriage. The pain of being married to an alcoholic and abusive husband may have temporarily distracted her, but it did not become a fatal distraction in her life.

Scripture tells us that Abigail was "a woman of good understanding" (1 Sam. 25:3), which meant that she was highly intelligent. She was smart, but more importantly, she was wise. The phrase *good understanding* implies that a person has something more than mere knowledge. The Book of Proverbs admonishes us to seek wisdom over knowledge: "Wisdom is the principal thing; therefore get wisdom: and with all thy getting get understanding" (Prov. 4:7). Abigail had more than just knowledge; she knew how to apply the knowledge she had gained and the common sense to operate successfully within her daily life circumstances. We might say that she knew what the "real deal" was and knew how to work around it. And in her marriage, that meant she knew and understood what kind of man her husband was, and she tried to work with him to the best of her ability.

In addition to Abigail's wisdom, the Bible tells us that she was "of a beautiful countenance" (1 Sam. 25:3). This meant more than that she had a pretty face. The word *countenance* takes into account a person's entire image, including her personality. She may have been pretty, yes, but she was also pleasant. Her attractiveness came from the inside out. This is also a significant point because, as we will see as we look at her situation, Abigail had found a way of not letting her husband's issues affect in a negative way. She did not "wear" her unhappy marriage on her person.

Don't we all know women who reveal by their countenance everything that is going wrong in the significant relationships in their lives? We can see the distraction in their eyes, their demeanor and their body language. But because Abigail refused to let Nabal's "issues" take away her beautiful countenance, she was already well on her way to avoiding this potentially fatal distraction.

Let's take a look at this husband of hers. The Bible tells us that Abigail was married to a very wealthy man named Nabal. The name Nabal is significant. In biblical times, the name of a person was often a reflection of the character of the person bearing that name. A person's name also gave insight into their destiny; it even reflected the gifts that a person had or the flaws they possessed. Earlier, in the Book of Genesis, Jacob's name, which meant "trickster" or "supplanter," foreshadowed his future deceitful actions, especially his disinheritance of his brother, Esau, by trickery.

The same is true of Abigail's husband, Nabal, whose name means "churl." That is an ancient word that means "angry, violent, loud-mouthed and insulting; a hard to please person."[1] The Bible further describes Nabal as being "very drunken" (1 Sam. 25:36). In modern terms, we would describe Nabal as an alcoholic or a substance abuser. He is the prototype of a violent and, at the very least, verbally abusive husband.

Many godly women today can relate to the pain of being married to a substance-abusing spouse. The term *substance abuser* brings to mind someone who cannot be trusted to keep his word about controlling or quitting his addictive behaviors. It implies someone who wastes the family's resources on his own selfish practices. It describes the demoralizing cycle of sobriety followed by bouts of drunkenness or getting high on drugs—the cycle of hope followed by disappointment each time the substance abuser goes on a binge. It describes the millions of women who are living with husbands who are "addicted" to things other than alcohol. The addictive pattern is the same whether the behavior is gambling, legal or illegal drugs, alcohol, pornography or adultery. Truly any woman who has lived with a loved one caught in the grip of any one of these obsessive behaviors could testify with Abigail that an entire family can be brought to the brink of ruin by just one person's undisciplined and self-indulgent conduct. And any one of these behaviors is more than just a casual distraction; they can easily become relationship killers—in effect, a fatal distraction.

Many women can probably relate to the story of a beautiful young woman—godly, loving and well-mannered in every way—who finds herself "unequally yoked" to an angry, abusive addict. That could have been a distraction with a capital D! But as the story continues, we will see that although problems in relationships may distract us, no matter how painful they are, they do not have to become fatal distractions to us.

Despite his propensity for alcohol, Nabal was a wealthy rancher with extensive holdings of sheep on the open range. As was the case in the early days of our own western frontier, bands of outlaws and thieves roamed the countryside, raiding the camps of the herders and stealing the flocks, with their valuable fleece, and even killing the men who were herding them. At the time this story takes place, David, the future king of Israel, was living in the mountains and fighting against King Saul.

An entire family can be brought to the brink of ruin by just one person's undisciplined and self-indulgent conduct.

He had a band of six hundred men with him who, although branded as outlaws, cared for Nabal's shepherds who were nearby, seeing to it that no one harmed them or took their sheep.

David's men protected Nabal's far-flung herds, but when they needed provisions of food and other supplies, Nabal's response was surprising. David had sent a messenger to Nabal asking for a returned favor of food and supplies for the weary men who had protected his flocks and shepherds. Instead of being gracious and accommodating, as one would expect, Nabal was negative and insulting. He not only replied with an emphatic *no*, but he also said it in a belittling and demeaning way. Furious at Nabal's ingratitude and insults, David gathered four hundred of his armed men and declared that nothing and no one would be left alive on Nabal's ranch by morning—and that included Abigail.

Fortunately, Abigail had an advance warning of the impending crisis. Upon hearing from the messenger how Nabal had responded, in her wisdom she discerned that David was on his way to exact vengeance. Immediately, she prepared sheep dressed for the men to eat, wine, raisins, bread and cakes of figs—all of the things that David and his men could possibly need—and she prepared them by the wagonload. She rushed out to intercept David, and when she reached him, she threw herself at his feet, honoring him and speaking of the future he would have as a great warrior. She begged David to accept her gifts and turn from his intent for a bloody revenge. David's heart was softened by the penitent woman before him, and he relented. He accepted the gifts and commended Abigail for her wisdom in preventing a bloody massacre.

Proactive vs. Reactive

When Abigail returned to her husband's house to tell him what had happened, Nabal was in the midst of a drunken party, and Abigail chose to not tell him the story until the next day, when he finally sobered up. There is a significant lesson in this for women today: Abigail wisely *picked an opportune time to discuss a difficult matter with him.* Notice, she did not tell him what happened until the crisis was safely averted. She knew the man she was dealing with and that he had already refused David's request. There was nothing to be gained by arguing with him to change his mind or by railing at him and wringing her hands about the coming disaster. David's warriors would simply have overtaken them as they stood there arguing about whose fault it was!

Instead, Abigail became proactive rather than reactive. She actively sought to find a solution rather than wasting time placing blame. When we are caught in negative situations, it is so much better to determine what we can do—whether it is get out of the immediate danger or try to minimize the damage—instead of casting blame on someone else. Rather than staying in the same spot and being paralyzed by the

Rather than drowning in self-pity over what she didn't have, she focused on what resources she did have.

circumstances, Abigail was able to present her husband with a situation that was solved, settled and successfully handled. And when Nabal heard how close he had come to a violent death at the hands of David, the Bible says "his heart died within him, and he became as a stone" (2 Sam. 25:37). Nabal was dead within two weeks' time.

When David heard that Nabal had died and that Abigail was now a widow, he sent messengers back to gather her and her handmaids and bring them on the road with him and his growing army, and Abigail became David's wife. The story concludes with David's being crowned king of Judah in the southern city of Hebron. Abigail, the woman who was once locked in a marriage to a violent, drunken husband, had become a queen!

Abigail had every reason to be fatally distracted. Her husband was clearly a bad-tempered, violent and verbally abusive man. He was an alcoholic who was selfish, ungrateful and unfair. A lifetime of living in such an emotional climate could have clearly destroyed Abigail's destiny. Many of us, in that situation, would have indulged in a lifelong pity-party, crying "Poor me" or "Why me?" But Abigail's attitude and actions—her response to a bad situation—are what, in effect, changed her life circumstances.

Abigail did not complain. She did not even blame Nabal for what was going on. Instead, she clearly understood her husband and his limitations. And she worked with those limitations, even taking up the slack herself when the family was in crisis. Rather than drowning in self-pity over what she didn't have, she focused on what resources she did have. A proactive response beats a reactive one every time!

Look for the good in your situation. Look for the solution, and stay positive. Even when you pray over a problem, woman of God, it isn't always productive to keep rehearsing and rehashing the problem to God. He already knows the situation! It is more important to pray the Word of God over the problem. Repeat the promises of God about the problem. In taking this positive, proactive response, you will increase your own faith, which in turn will produce the desired result.

Think about it: proactive or reactive. Which will you choose? The power of a positive response to the most negative of circumstances brought Abigail out of a situation full of despair and into a promising new life.

CHAPTER 7

Elderly Parents: The Devotion of Ruth and Naomi

IF YOU ARE a middle-aged adult and your parents are still alive, at some point you will likely face the heartbreak and difficulties that come with watching them grow older. Although my own father died when I was seventeen, I am blessed because my mother is yet alive. At seventy-eight, she is the family matriarch, still the glue that holds my four brothers, two sisters and me together. But as is the nature of life, her advanced years have brought sickness and affliction, and my siblings and I take pride in keeping her comfortable and able to enjoy her life. During this time, I am grateful for the strong support system that comes from being in a large family.

Even under the best of circumstances, taking care of elderly parents can provide a major distraction to our walk with God. So many issues seem to arise at one time. There is the inevitability of your parent's aging and ultimate mortality, and the distress it causes for both them and you. And depending upon your parents' health, there may be multiple tasks involved in caring for them as they age: prescriptions to be filled, doctor's visits to take them on, health insurance forms to fill out.

In addition to all of this, there is also the paradoxical

and heartbreaking reversal of roles, which is difficult for both parents and daughter: The child they once nurtured and took care of is suddenly nurturing and caring for them.

I will always remember how devastated I was when I finally realized and admitted to myself that my own mother was actually growing old and would not be with me forever. I remember how I wept and cried—and my eyes are tearing up even as I write this. We do not realize what a strong foundation of security and support our parents and grandparents have given us until bit by bit, the structure they provided is weakened and eventually taken away.

Even under the best of circumstances, taking care of elderly parents can provide a major distraction to our walk with God.

While the emotional distress of dealing with aging parents is usually the most difficult aspect of the crisis, the sheer logistics of taking on their care and provision is an enormous task. In middle-age, our lives are already "maxed out" with jobs, spouses, children, church work and other activities, and adding the care and responsibility of elderly parents to this mix can cause our lives to literally strain at the seams.

God knows the struggles that we face, and He cares. He has spoken to us in His Word and shares His attitude toward the elderly in Leviticus 19:32, which reads: "Thou shalt rise up before the hoary head, and honour the face of the old man, and fear thy God: I am the LORD."

God equates the honor of the elderly with a fear and reverence of Him, and this directive was not taken lightly among the children of Israel. Our natural familial love should make the devotion, care and concern we have for our parents unquestionable—if we honor God, we should automatically honor our parents as well. It is in a woman's nature especially to nurture and care for people—not only the young, but also the weak, the sick and the elderly. This is so inherent in a woman's makeup that many women care for people who are not even their own blood relations!

A sweet illustration of a woman's care for her aging parent comes to us from the Book of Ruth, where we find the older woman, Naomi, bereft of her husband and her two sons. Although the family was originally from Israel, they had been living in the land of Moab when the men died. At that time, Naomi determined that she would return to her homeland—with or without her daughters-in-law, Orpah and Ruth. Orpah decided to part company with Naomi, but Ruth possessed a sense of care and responsibility so strong that she refused to leave Naomi's side. Even Naomi's warning that to follow her might cause her to remain husbandless did not deter Ruth from her commitment. Setting aside her need for future security and the love she had for her homeland, Moab, Ruth made one of the strongest declarations of loyalty and fidelity found in Scripture:

> Entreat me not to leave you, or to turn back from following after you; for wherever you go, I will go; and wherever you lodge, I will lodge; your people shall be my people, and your God, my God.
>
> —RUTH 1:16, NKJV

It is the same depth of determination expressed in this passage by Ruth that fuels the distraction many of us face as we care for our elderly parents. When our love for them is great, we will focus a great amount of our time and energy into securing and maintaining their well-being. And though this is an honorable pursuit, we must exercise care not to let the task overwhelm us.

God equates the honor of the elderly with a fear and reverence of Him.

A FAMILY AFFAIR

If a support system is available to you, utilize it. Try to involve all of your siblings in the process, and allow them to share in the responsibilities. Don't try to be a superhero, trying to do it all yourself and becoming so enmeshed in your parents' care that you shut everyone else out.

I once knew of a situation in which the oldest sibling in the family tried to care for her parents all by herself, but in so doing, she prevented her brothers and sisters from participating in the blessing of honoring their parents. Resentment at being left out of the process began to breed among her siblings, and what should have been a joint family effort that brought them together became instead a situation fraught with tension and animosity. An unfortunate by-product of the extreme sheltering by the daughter was that her mother mistakenly began to believe that the other children did not care about her! Fortunately, a trusted family member intervened in the nick of time and was able to effect peace and reconciliation within that family.

Perhaps your situation is a little different than the one I just described. Maybe you have been designated as the "Unofficial Family Caretaker," perhaps because you are single or have no children. For whatever reason, you always seem to be the one to take your parents to their doctor appointments, fill their prescriptions or run their errands. The bulk of the responsibility has been placed upon your shoulders.

If you have siblings, your parents' care should not be your sole responsibility. Explain to your brothers and sisters that your mother and father are parents to each of you, and they should pitch in. But take care that in this conversation you do not lay a guilt trip on your siblings. For a godly person, taking care of elderly parents is a responsibility that should be looked upon with honor and even a sense of joy.

You must learn how to maintain a healthy balance as you fulfill your family duties so that you do not become burned out in mind, body, spirit and attitude. The emotional toll that taking care of elderly parents can take on you is often subtle, and you may not be aware of all the effects. As your stress levels rise, you may experience difficulty sleeping. Or you may resort to unhealthy and destructive coping mechanisms to help you deal with the reality of your parents' impending mortality—overeating, loss of appetite, lack of focus or crying spells, just to name a few.

One friend told me that at times, when dealing with her elderly parents, she had to take pains to keep a grip on her temper. She would become irritated or even disgusted with them when they moved too slowly or did not appear to understand what she was trying to say to them.

"I felt so *badly*," she said to me, tears welling up in her eyes. "After all, this was *my mom* I found myself snapping at!"

When you feel yourself becoming irritated, take a deep breath. If you can, step away for a moment and regain your composure. If you are normally a calm person, your irritability could be a sign that your stress level has gotten too high, and you need a break from the situation. Try to get someone else to fill in for you, and take a little time away from the situation to clear your mind and get a handle on your emotions. Realize that your anger is not really at your parent; it is more likely at the frustration and pain of coping with the situation.

> **Maintain a healthy balance as you fulfill your family duties so that you do not become burned out in mind, body, spirit and attitude.**

Most of all, commit your frustration, anger and sadness to God, who understands your deepest hurts. Indeed, the Scripture encourages us in Hebrews 4:15–16:

> For we have not an high priest which cannot be touched with the feeling of our infirmities; but was in all points tempted like as we are, yet without sin. Let us therefore come boldly unto the throne of grace, that we may obtain mercy, and find grace to help in time of need.

Rest assured, God will give you the grace and help you need to lovingly cope with the heart-wrenching distraction of caring for your elderly parents.

With all the advances in technology, mankind has been afforded a longer and longer life span. Consequently, taking care of aging parents is a reality that most of us will eventually have to face. Care for yours to the best of your ability, and avail yourself of the grace and strength that God will give you during that time. As long as your parents are alive, enjoy them, and realize that their presence in your life is a blessing from God. If your parents have already gone on to be with the Lord, praise God for their lives, for the time you did get to spend with them, and look for the opportunity to be a blessing in the life of some elderly person who may be feeling lonely and neglected.

God rewarded Ruth for her allegiance, honor and faithfulness to Naomi. He will bless and reward you as well.

SECTION 2

EIGHT FATAL DISTRACTIONS

CHAPTER 8

Fatal Distractions: The Subtle Killers

FATAL DISTRACTIONS: THE SUBTLE KILLERS

IN THE FIRST section of this book, we looked at some situations that would certainly be troubling for the women involved, but these situations didn't necessarily cause a fatal distraction and cause the women to become sidetracked from God's plan for their lives. The reason for this is that those situations were actually external circumstances in the person's life—that is, the situation could have been altered by the person's response to it and through God's intervention. But the next set of problems we will look at are more insidious—they are caused by harmful attitudes and internal dispositions that at first may seem unimportant—even trivial—but when allowed to continue, they slowly degrade the influence of God in our lives and become a fatal distraction.

God is warning us not to be pulled from our spiritual destiny by these fatal distractions. Let's reexamine Mark 4:3–8, 13–19, looking at it in The Amplified Bible:

> Give attention to this! Behold, a sower went out to sow. And as he was sowing, some seed fell along the path, and the birds came and ate it up.
>
> Other seed [of the same kind] fell on ground full of rocks, where it had not much soil; and at

once it sprang up, because it had no depth of soil; and when the sun came up, it was scorched, and because it had not taken root, it withered away.

Other seed [of the same kind] fell among thorn plants, and the thistles grew and pressed together and utterly choked and suffocated it, and it yielded no grain.

And other seed [of the same kind] fell into good (well-adapted) soil and brought forth grain, growing up and increasing, and yielded up to thirty times as much, and sixty times as much, and even a hundred times as much as had been sown...

And He said to them...The sower sows the Word.

The ones along the path are those who have the Word sown [in their hearts], but when they hear, Satan comes at once and [by force] takes away the message which is sown in them.

And in the same way the ones sown upon stony ground are those who, when they hear the Word, at once receive and accept and welcome it with joy; and they have no real root in themselves, and so they endure for a little while; then when trouble or persecution arises on account of the Word, they immediately are offended (become displeased, indignant, resentful) and they stumble and fall away.

And the ones sown among the thorns are others who hear the Word; then the cares and anxieties of the world and distractions of the age, and the pleasure and delight and false glamour and deceitfulness of riches, and the craving and passionate desire for other things creep in and choke and suffocate the Word, and it becomes fruitless.

Fatal Distractions: The Subtle Killers

In the parable, Jesus was teaching His disciples about the importance of the Word. It is not enough to have a Bible on your bookshelf; you must take the time and effort to read the Word and cause it to be productive and fruitful in *you*. In the story, a sower went out to plant his seeds. As he was casting the seed about, some fell on stony ground, some fell among the thorns and weeds, some fell by the wayside, and some fell on good ground.

Each of the environments in which the seeds fell was significant to Jesus' story. Those seeds that fell by the wayside were devoured by the birds of the air. They never took root. They never grew. They were eaten or destroyed before their potential could even be harvested for the benefit of the farmer. Those that fell on stony ground sprouted quickly, but because of the shallowness of the soil, no roots could develop, and the sun scorched the plant before it could reach its seed-bearing potential. The stony ground is indicative of the "stony" hearts of some of God's people: The seeds of the Word never reproduce themselves into fruit-bearing plants, and the result is a profitless ministry.

Despite the distressing outcome of these first two types of soil, the most tragic of all were the "lost" seeds— the wasted or unprofitable seeds that had fallen among weeds and thorns. These seeds did take root and sprout. These seeds had the potential to grow into ripened fruit, which in turn would bear more seeds, reproduce itself and be profitable to the sower. But look at the sad result:

> The cares and anxieties of the world and distractions of the age, and the pleasure and delight and false glamour and deceitfulness of

> riches, and the craving and passionate desire
> for other things creep in and choke and suffo-
> cate the Word, and it becomes fruitless.
> —MARK 4:19, AMP

The Word of God was smothered by the distractions of life, and these became fatal distractions to the person's God-given potential.

Most of us realize that God has ordained a path for each of our lives, but how often do we consider that our journey is not completely for our own benefit? God has ordained your life to have purpose *for* Him. The Word is not birthed in you only for your convenience or to bless you with a life of comfort and leisure. The Word is planted in your spirit to bring forth fruit in the lives of the people with whom you come into con-

> It is not enough to have a Bible on your bookshelf; you must take the time and effort to read the Word and cause it to be productive and fruitful in you.

tact! Now, it is true that following God's plan is what will bring you the greatest satisfaction and sense of purpose, but it does require a life of obedience and commitment. The Word must be so fruitful in you that it inspires you to do God's will with fervor, passion and commitment.

Each of us has a circle of influence made up of the people God has called us to minister to or influence. God has given each of us gifts for ministry that have a specific place, purpose and design in His master plan, and we must trust God to be faithful and bring about His purpose. Our job is to be faithful to nurture and water the seed He has entrusted to us and avoid the many fatal distractions Satan would try to throw in our path.

LET'S MEET THE CONTESTANTS!

Women in particular are susceptible to the subtle yet insidious distractions that "dress themselves up" to be something beautiful, yet inside are rotten to the core. Imagine a beauty contest—much like the Miss America pageant that takes place in our country every year. Imagine there are eight contestants—each one more shapely and beautiful than the last. Their faces are made up with the finest cosmetics, their evening gowns glitter with sequins, and each displays a banner over the shoulder that tells her special category of deception.

Behind the stage curtain, Satan is directing the show. He lines them up and, one by one, sends them out before the crowd: *Envy* is first, followed by *Loneliness* and then *Anger*. The crowd cheers, and Satan smiles as members of the audience begin to consider just how attractive the contestants are. Not to be outdone, *Bitterness*, *Hurt* and *Fear* strut across the stage. And the crowd gasps when *Rejection* makes her entrance—she has been a favorite among audience members for years. But Satan has saved the "best" for last: The most captivating contestant of all wears a banner that simply reads, "*Yourself.*" This potential distraction stops the judges in their tracks, and the hands-down winner is declared. She is there when you get up in the morning, when you're driving in your car alone, every time you look in the mirror. No one could deny that *Yourself* was the most attractive distraction of them all.

Fatal Distractions

One of the problems with fatal distractions is that we consider them as if they were the truth set in stone, sometimes even saying, "Well, that's just a part of my personality." But this is NOT true! Distractions are lies from the pit of hell. They are sent by Satan to pull you away from your destiny and take you down a side road that the devil has designed for you. You will never reach your destination from a "detour" path. But the distraction will come to you and whisper in your ear, "You need to go another way so you can be accepted, so you can be loved, so you can be famous, or rich, or happy, or feel important, or be a part of the 'in crowd.'" But this is not true—you *don't* need to succumb to the dictates of the world in order to find fulfillment, purpose, joy or even the desires of your heart.

The distraction tries to tell you, "Take the easy way out." Most of us would like to avoid conflict, pain and sacrifice. We don't like to take risks—but there is a cost of discipleship, a price you must pay for the anointing in your life.

Fatal distractions will not show up in your life as obvious sins with terrible outcomes to be avoided. In the movie *Fatal Attraction*, Alex was a beautiful and desirable woman. She was an "attractive" distraction that drew the man away from his wife and family. That is the subtlety of the trap that Satan sets for God's anointed ones. The distraction is easily embraced. It does not repel us. It may seem to make sense with what is going on in our lives. It may even be "justifiable," but it is a fatal distraction just the same.

A compelling example of such a distraction can be found in the confrontation between Jesus and Peter in Matthew 16. Jesus was distressed because, although He had been ministering for three years among the people, His disciples still did not seem to have a clear understanding of His true purpose. They had seen Him feed more than five thousand people on more than one occasion—with just a few fish and loaves of bread. They had seen Him cleanse the lepers and cast out the legion of demons in the lunatic in the tombs. They had seen Him defy the laws of nature by walking on water. They had seen Him call Lazarus from the tomb, reversing the course of inevitable decay in a body that had been dead four days. They had seen Him heal the lame and the blind. They knew beyond a shadow of a doubt that no one could do these miracles unless He had been empowered by God—that He was indeed the promised Messiah.

> Distractions are lies from the pit of hell. They are sent by Satan to pull you away from your destiny and take you down a side road that the devil has designed for you.

But if the disciples, who were for the most part unlearned men, did not understand the full meaning of Jesus' purpose on the earth, surely the religious leaders would: They had studied the Scriptures. They knew the prophecies. They knew the signs that would confirm the identity of the coming Messiah. They had also seen the dove descending at His baptism and heard the voice from heaven proclaiming, "This is my beloved Son, in whom I am well pleased" (Matt. 3:17).

Knowing that His time of death was approaching, Jesus yearned for affirmation from those around Him, and

His heart groaned as He asked the question of His disciples, "Whom do men say that I the Son of Man am?" (Matt. 16:13). Would they understand the true meaning of His mission on earth?

The disciples replied, "Some say that thou art John the Baptist: some, Elias; and others, Jeremias, or one of the prophets" (v. 14).

Jesus then asked, "But whom say ye that I am?" (v. 15).

Peter's affirmation has become one of the cornerstones of the Christian faith. In his typical brash style, Peter proclaimed with confidence, "Thou art the Christ, the Son of the living God" (v. 16). Jesus was so pleased with Peter's response that He commended him by giving him a new name and a new destiny as the foundation of God's holy church: "And I say also unto thee, That thou art Peter [Petros], and upon this rock I will build my church; and the gates of hell shall not prevail against it" (v. 18).

> A distraction in the purest sense of the word is anything or anyone that pulls you away from your God-ordained purpose.

This is one of the most empowering commissions in the entire Bible! Peter could not have had a more "spiritual" moment with his Lord, but in the very next moment, Peter became Jesus' most dangerous fatal distraction. How quickly attitudes can change!

When Jesus told His disciples that He was about to go to Jerusalem to be betrayed and crucified, Peter erupted in denial: "Lord, surely You don't have to die that way!" Jesus could read between the lines all of the temptations that

Peter had left unsaid: "No, Jesus. You don't have to fulfill the destiny that God ordained for You before the foundation of the world." "You don't have to suffer the agony of crucifixion." "There has to be an easier way, a better way, a different way to get the job done."

But thankfully Jesus could see Peter's assertion for what it really was: a distraction in the purest sense of the word—anything or anyone that pulls you away from your God-ordained purpose. Jesus immediately responded, "Get thee behind me, Satan!" (v. 23). In that moment, He identified the true source of every fatal distraction. The entire plan of salvation was hung in the balance with Jesus' reaction to Peter's suggestion. The human race would never have been saved if Jesus had followed that one fatal distraction. The plan that had been set forth in Genesis just after the Fall of Adam and Eve would have been short-circuited and would never have reached fulfillment if Jesus had listened to His "friend" in that moment. Thank God He did not!

Fatal distractions are subtle. They appear on the surface to be beneficial, to be benign. They may even be presented by a friend. They may seem to meet the need of the moment, but if followed to their conclusion, they bring forth death: the death of the anointing and the divine purpose and plan for your life.

CHAPTER 9

Envy and Jealousy

KING SAUL, THE first king of Israel, seemed to have everything going for him. He was tall, handsome, wealthy and the most powerful man in his nation. He would seem to be in the least likely position to suffer the fatal distraction of envy—if anything, it seemed as if people should be jealous of him!

However, that was not the case, and jealousy—King Saul's fatal flaw—wreaked havoc in his life and in the lives of those around him, and eventually it cost him his kingdom.

The seeds of jealousy first took root in King Saul when he and his newly appointed armorbearer, David, returned from the battle against Goliath. Saul had been so impressed with David's character, demeanor and performance that not only had he made him his armorbearer, but also he had promoted him as captain over his men of war. All went well until their return, and they heard the women praising their war effort in song:

> And the women responded as they laughed and frolicked, saying, Saul has slain his thousands, and David his ten thousands.
> —1 SAMUEL 18:7, AMP

FATAL DISTRACTIONS

At that moment Saul allowed the seed of his fatal distraction to sprout in his mind. Any previous agenda in Saul's life was exchanged for a new one: that of destroying David's life.

Perhaps the reason Saul was so susceptible to this distraction is that he evidently suffered from a sense of poor self-worth. If he had been secure in the divine appointment given to him by God, he would have had no reason to be jealous. Always know, dear sister, that there is more than enough of the provision and blessings of God to go around—what God bestows upon another in no way will take away from what He promises to give to you. Yes, God had given David the victory over Goliath, but David's cutting off the giant's head in no way made Saul any less the king of Israel. Many people are like Saul—as long as God is blessing and exalting them, their lives are serene and secure. But when God begins to pour out His blessings, anointing and power upon others, they take on what I call a "monopoly mentality"—they act as if the favor and blessings of God should belong exclusively to them! What soon follows is a spirit of judgment, just as what occurred in Saul's life: Upon hearing the song of the women, he said, "They have ascribed unto David ten thousands, and to me they have ascribed but thousands: *and what can he have more but the kingdom?*" (1 Sam. 18:8, emphasis added).

A spirit of judgment will make you say to yourself, *Who does she think she is? She thinks she's all that.* Or, *What did she do to deserve that? I know someone who deserves it more!* Instead of concentrating on what God is doing for you and reflecting upon what He has promised to you, you jealously zero in on what He is doing for someone else.

If, like Saul, you lose sight of what God is doing in your own life, you will eventually fall victim to the same mistake he made: that of focusing your time, attention and energy on trying to circumvent what God is doing in the life of someone else. Instead of directing your will to conform to the will of the Father and pursue those things that will bring spiritual increase to your life, you become mean, spiteful and even manipulative—a tool in the hands of the devil, whose intent is to steal, kill and destroy the life of every believer.

Saul justified his jealousy and ill will toward David by convincing himself that the leadership of his kingdom was in jeopardy. Even though David had only demonstrated loyalty to Saul and a desire to uphold and protect his king and his country, Saul's insecurity caused him to misread David's intentions. It is the trick of the enemy to cause us to see our brothers and sisters in Christ as our adversaries!

> **What God bestows upon another in no way will take away from what He promises to give to you.**

In addition to stemming from a sense of inadequacy and low self-worth, Saul's behaviors and attitudes were rooted in fear: the fear of being replaced, the fear of being outdone, the fear that his acceptance by others would diminish, the fear that God would give to another more than He had given to him. It is not the will of God that we fall prey to being driven by thoughts of inadequacy or fear!

First Corinthians 1:30 tells us, "But of him are ye in Christ Jesus, who of God is made unto us wisdom, and righteousness, and sanctification, and redemption." Our sufficiency cannot come from within ourselves; it comes from Christ, "that filleth all in all" (Eph. 1:23). He is in us, and in Him, there is no inadequacy or lack! When we allow ourselves to lose focus on the move of God in our own lives and become fatally distracted by the blessings of others, we are more prone to forget that everything we need—and everything we are and are to be—is in Christ. Don't allow the devil to trick you into striving to maintain a position. Strive to maintain the will of Christ in your life, and everything else will follow.

THE DIFFERENCE BETWEEN JEALOUSY AND ENVY

The *Merriam-Webster Dictionary* defines jealousy as "a jealous disposition, attitude, or feeling."[1] The state of being jealous is defined as being "hostile toward a rival or one believed to enjoy an advantage."[2] What is immediately disturbing about this definition is the fact that it contains the word *rival.* It should go without saying that it is a trick of the enemy for sisters in the body of Christ to view one another as rivals! How is it, woman of God, that we feel we have to *strive against* one another rather than *work with* one another for the kingdom of God? A rival is one who strives for a competitive advantage over another—but are we not on the same team? If we are on the same team, shouldn't our striving be for the good of the team—that the members of the kingdom of God be enhanced, uplifted and strengthened? Unfortunately, the fatal distraction of jealousy has infected a large portion of the body of Christ, and too much of the energy we should be expending to advance God's kingdom is being wasted on the fallout that arises from giving place to jealousy.

As opposed to jealousy, the word *envy* is defined as "painful or resentful awareness of an advantage enjoyed by another, joined with a desire to possess the same advantage."[3] The first thing that stands out to me in that definition is that envy involves "a *painful* awareness." Imagine that! A by-product of envy is *pain*: pain at the thought of someone else's enjoyment of something you don't possess—whether it

> Inordinate desires lead to inordinate actions, which are damaging to both the person inflicting the actions and the persons against whom they are inflicted.

be spiritual or physical, tangible or intangible. This directly contradicts Scripture, which tells us to "rejoice with them that do rejoice," not to be *pained* by the knowledge of their blessings!

The second compelling characteristic of envy is that in addition to causing pain, it brings the *desire to possess the same advantage.* Because this desire stems from envy, we would call it an "inordinate desire," one that is not sanctioned by God. *Inordinate desires*—desires that fall out of the will of God and are against the law of love—lead to inordinate actions, which are damaging to both the person inflicting the actions and the persons against whom they are inflicted.

Have you distinguished the marked difference between envy and jealousy? Jealousy causes *hostility* toward those whom we view as rivals, those we believe enjoy an advantage that we don't have. But envy takes it one step further: It carries a *desire to possess the same advantage*. In other words, when I'm jealous, I'm hostile to another person because they have something that I don't have. When I'm envious, I am painfully aware of the other's advantage, and I have the desire to possess the same advantage.

Can you see these patterns in your own life? It can be frightening when you think about it, can't it? Yet it is such an everyday reality that it cannot be ignored. Too many lives are being lived in the shadow of these vile, pernicious emotions. Not only must we address this matter, but also we must conquer and eradicate it!

COMBATING ENVY AND JEALOUSY

How do envy and jealousy take root in the first place? We allow them to become strongholds in our lives when we fail to avail ourselves of the sufficiency that is ours in Christ. We either don't know it's available, we don't exercise the strength of will to appropriate it, or we don't believe we can successfully utilize the principles and promises contained in the Word. We are told in 2 Peter 1:2–3:

> Grace and peace be multiplied unto you through the knowledge of God, and of Jesus our Lord, according as his divine power hath given unto us all things that pertain unto life and godliness, through the knowledge of him that hath called us to glory and virtue.

According to Peter, grace and peace can be multiplied to us through an increased knowledge, understanding and awareness of God and of our Lord and Savior Jesus Christ.

Now while the world would say, "A little knowledge is a dangerous thing," I would say, "A *lack of* knowledge is a dangerous thing!" You can't live any better than you *know* how to live, and being ignorant of the promises and provisions of God will set you up for failure. You cannot fully be the person that God would have you to be without knowing who and what He says you can be.

Consider the affirmation of Romans 8:16–17: "The Spirit itself beareth witness with our spirit, that we are the children of God: and if children, then heirs; heirs of God, and joint-heirs with Christ." Being a "joint-heir" makes me privy to not only everything that Jesus has, but also to everything that He is! So often we dwell upon the physical, material and tangible things we stand to receive by knowing and being in Christ, but the spiritual benefits far outweigh these earthly things. In Ephesians 1:3, Paul stated, "Blessed be the God and Father of our Lord Jesus Christ, who hath blessed us with all spiritual blessings in heavenly places in Christ." The most profitable blessings that our Father God bestows upon us are spiritual blessings in Christ. In fact, the spiritual blessings that come from knowing and being in Christ are actually the blessings that we should be pursuing!

"Seek ye first the kingdom of God, and his righteousness," Jesus said, "and *all these things* shall be added unto

> Instead of focusing upon these carnal things and spending so much time and energy in their pursuit, center your attention on obtaining the greater spiritual things that "being in Christ" affords.

you" (Matt. 6:33, emphasis added). What "things" is He speaking of? Food, clothing and shelter—those material and tangible things that He said the world seeks after. According to Jesus, this was not an acceptable pattern of behavior for a child of God! But if you live as He wants you to live, He promises that the material blessings will *automatically* follow. Instead of focusing upon these carnal things and spending so much time and energy in their pursuit, center your attention on obtaining the greater spiritual things that "being in Christ" affords.

Every godly character trait that we lack or need is in Him. Paul wrote, "But of him are ye in Christ Jesus, who of God is made unto us wisdom, and righteousness, and sanctification, and redemption" (1 Cor. 1:30). What woman of God is there that does not want to be wise, righteous, sanctified and redeemed? These are all spiritual attributes and blessings, and they come through a relationship with Christ.

TAKE A LOOK IN THE MIRROR

Tell me, are your thoughts and behaviors toward fellow believers less than what your heavenly Father would have them to be? Is there someone whom you are "eying jealously," as Saul did? Is there a brother or sister whom you perceive to be a threat to your position? Although the position may well have been given to you by God, it is not His will that you become possessive and territorial—the way a dog guards a bone! God is the One who opens doors that no man can shut, as Revelation 3:8 states, and nothing He gives you can be taken from you *except* by His divine permission. If He *ordained* it, then He will *sustain* you in it—rest assured of that!

Ask yourself this question: "Is there someone in the body of Christ to whom I have been directing an *undue amount* of attention, someone to whom I have been comparing myself or even with whom I have been competing?" Often, when you fall into the same trap that Saul fell in, you become competitive, self-seeking and self-promoting. Are you engaging in "power plays" or attempting to do things that will upstage your perceived opponent? If you are, then watch out! That is not a mandate of God but a mission of the devil! The apostle James wrote:

> If ye have bitter envying and strife in your hearts, glory not, and lie not against the truth. This wisdom descendeth not from above, but is earthly, sensual, devilish. For where envying and strife is, there is confusion and every evil work.
>
> —JAMES 3:14–16

Saul's repeated plots, schemes and attempts to take David's life marred his life. While you may not be going so far as to cause a person's *physical* death, are you guilty of activities that undermine their *spiritual* life, well-being or ministry? Are you spreading rumors, gossip or slander, undermining their authority or their agenda, or seeking to destroy their influence with others? In some ways, these detrimental activities can be deadlier than the sharpest knife. If his natural life were taken, that believer would simply go on to be with the Lord. But if his influence is destroyed or his name smeared, the effects of such carnal sabotage can have far-reaching consequences that will linger for many years. Far be it for any professed child of God to engage in such behavior! Indeed, "let no corrupt communication proceed out of your mouth, but that which is good to the use of edifying…Let all bitterness, and wrath, and anger, and clamour, and evil speaking, be put away from you, with all malice: and be ye kind one to another, tenderhearted" (Eph. 4:29, 31–32).

Remember, woman of God, if the role you are in is one that was given to you by God, then that is a blessed place, an honorable role. One godly pastor I know used to say, "True success is being in the perfect will of God." We may lose sight of that fact when the place we are in is not glamorous, or we feel unappreciated. Detrimental thoughts come into our minds, and we feel overlooked, undervalued and unappreciated. "What good does it do me to be who I am?" we rage, and look with envious, resentful eyes at those we perceive to be better off than ourselves. If we fail to cast down these hurtful, self-defeating and negative thoughts, they soon take root in our verbal affirmations and actions, and instead of maintaining our confidence in the good plans and purposes of God, holding fast to the assurance that in due time God will exalt us, we resort to our own devices.

Granted, I understand that there are times in your life when you may become dissatisfied with what you are doing and where you are going. A *healthy* dissatisfaction will always lead to positive growth. But the desire to "do better" or "go higher" in *any* realm—personal, professional or spiritual—should *never* be at the expense of someone else's well-being or your own. Those quests that are *godly* in origin and nature will never cause us to violate the biblical principles clearly articulated in the Word of God, and it will not cause us to resort to the types of activities outlined by the apostle James:

> What causes fights and quarrels among you? Don't they come from your desires that battle within you? You want something but don't get it. You kill and covet, but you cannot have what you want. You quarrel and fight. You do not have, because you do not ask God. When you ask, you do not receive, because you ask with wrong motives, that you may spend what you get on your pleasures.
>
> —JAMES 4:1–3, NIV

Woman of God, what drives you? Do you have a longing for the deeper things of God—to be the whole, complete, fulfilled vessel of ministry that you know you were meant to be? Do you keep your heart, mind and spirit ready for a move of God in your life, your ears attuned for the Spirit's slightest whisper or call?

What drives you? Does the presence of God still inspire you, overwhelm you and fill you with awe? As the deer pants for the water brook, does your soul reach out for more of God? Do you find your thoughts drifting heavenward during the course of the day? Do passages of Scripture or the words of a gospel song enter your mind as you go about your day? Or sadly, are you more like Saul—your thoughts centered on how you can "get ahead" and jealous of anyone who you feel is "standing in your way"?

Precious handmaiden of God, can you remember what your spirit was like before envy and jealousy maligned and disfigured it? Do you remember the joy you experienced when you heard testimonies of victory, the agreement you experienced when words of truth were ministered by a colaborer in the gospel?

If you have been bound by the distractions of envy and jealousy, I hope that you will cry out to God in repentance and allow Him to set you back on the path toward His will in your life.

TWO SIDES OF THE COIN

Both sides of the coin of envy and jealousy are deadly. On the one hand, I've encountered scores of women who have been ensnared by envy and jealousy, and they are simply miserable. But the "flip side" of the coin is the woman who has been the *victim* of someone who was entangled by these fatal distractions.

A woman who has been on the *receiving end* of an envious, jealous person has borne the brunt of malicious and destructive forces that have the potential to destroy her life. She may have suffered loss of influence, if the jealous one has slandered her name. She may have dealt with whispers, rumors and false accusations, or been presented in a negative light and misjudged. If she's in ministry, she may have had to stand before people and minister under the burden of fighting off condemnation—not from *God*, but from the people in the audience who were judging her falsely.

> If the role you are in is one that was given to you by God, then that is a blessed place, an honorable role.

On which side of the coin would you fall? Which

woman are you? Are you the jealous, envious and spiteful one—the person being used by the enemy to steal the happiness and effectiveness of others? Or are you the innocent victim, wearied by the battle but determined to walk in victory?

If you have been a victim, I wholeheartedly pray that you have allowed God to sustain and keep you. But if you have responded negatively or in an un-Christlike manner to the evil winds of envy and jealousy that have blown your way, repent. Reaffirm to yourself that "the weapons of our warfare are not carnal, but mighty through God to the pulling down of strong holds" (2 Cor. 10:4). Ask God to infuse you with love for the individuals who have been persecuting you. Realize that Jesus said:

> Blessed are ye, when men shall revile you, and persecute you, and shall say all manner of evil against you falsely, for my sake. Rejoice, and be exceeding glad: for great is your reward in heaven: for so persecuted they the prophets which were before you.
> —MATTHEW 5:11–12

If you are on the other side of the coin—guilty of being the envious and jealous one, I urge you to repent before God at this very moment. Acknowledge before Him the sinful attitudes in your life. Understand that the enemy has been using your attitude to steal from, kill and destroy others. But know above all else that God loves you, and that the beat of His heart is to bring deliverance and restoration to your life. He is your Shepherd, and you will never lack any good thing because He is your all in all. The fullness of everything that He is, my sister, is already yours, so there is no need to covet the possessions, position or influence of another individual. You are a daughter of God, you are made in His image and likeness, you are the apple of His eye—and in Him there is no lack. There is more than enough of Him for you and for the other members of the body of Christ.

As you repent before God and allow Him to cleanse, purify and restore you, I would encourage you to take it one step further. In Luke 19, when Jesus paid a visit to the house of Zacchaeus, Zacchaeus repented and made a promise to Him: "Lord, the half of my goods I give to the poor; and if I have taken any thing from any man by false accusation, I restore him fourfold" (v. 8). If you are truly repentant, you will take it one step further and ask God to help you bring restoration to the lives of those you have hurt. Although they may be a little wary of your overtures at first (and rightfully so, wouldn't you say?), if your repentance is genuine and your desire to make amends is heartfelt,

> You are a daughter of God, you are made in His image and likeness, you are the apple of His eye— and in Him there is no lack.

the underlying motives of your pure heart will soon be evident. Once that is done, continue to follow God's plan for you, resisting the distractions of envy and jealousy. As Paul wrote in Galatians 5:1, "Stand fast therefore in the liberty wherewith Christ hath made [you] free, and be not entangled again with the yoke of bondage."

CHAPTER 10

Loneliness

Genesis 2:18 says, "Then the Lord God said, 'It is not good for the man to be alone'" (NAS). With these words, God confirmed the need for human relationships and began the process that would introduce the first relationship between two human beings.

In the creation of the world, God first created the perfect environment for mankind: He made the stars, the sun and moon, Planet Earth and everything in it—oceans, forests, birds, fish and other animals—and then He crafted His crowning creation: man. God created man to have dominion over everything else He had made, and He gave Adam the task of naming the animals as he saw fit. We do not know how long Adam resided in the garden alone, but we do know that as he was naming the animals, it struck him that none of the other creatures were like him—and in that sense, he was alone.

But God, Adam's loving Creator, had anticipated this need for human relationships, and as a result, Eve, the first woman, was lovingly crafted from a rib taken from Adam's side.

Can you imagine? Adam and Eve had a perfect relationship, unmarred by the taint of sin. Their communication, their commonality, was unhindered, as was their love for each other. Their relationship served as the springboard for all other human relationships that would follow: marital, familial, platonic, nonplatonic and the like. Man would never again be alone, for from the point of Eve's creation, there would always be more than one human being on the earth. But after the Fall, even though no man or woman would ever again be truly alone—the way that Adam had been—unfortunately, the concept of loneliness had entered the picture.

ALONE, BUT NOT LONELY

It is possible to be alone and feel completely happy and satisfied in one's heart. But it is also possible to be lonely in a crowd. To be *alone* is to be "separated from others: isolated, exclusive of anyone or anything else."[1] But *loneliness* is defined as "the state of being lonely, being without company, desolate, producing a feeling of bleakness or desolation."[2]

Being alone is primarily a physical reality; loneliness is a state of mind.

The word *alone* emphasizes more of a physical sense than the emotional involvement implied by the word *lonely*. When one is *solitary* (alone), it may indicate isolation as a chosen course, but when combined with the word *lonely*, it "suggests sadness and a sense of loss." The word *lonely* adds to a physical solitude a suggestion of longing for companionship.

In essence, being *alone* does not necessarily make one *lonely*, and being *lonely* does not necessarily come because one is *alone*. Being alone is primarily a physical reality; loneliness is a state of mind.

Loneliness becomes a fatal distraction when it leads to sadness, dejection and a sense of desolation that cause you to lose sight of the promise made by Jesus: "I will never leave thee, nor forsake thee" (Heb. 13:5).

You may be alone because of logistical factors: You may be single, have no children or may have just moved to a new city or community. But that doesn't mean you have to be lonely. Loneliness is largely dependent upon where you are mentally, not physically. A woman can be married, have a house full of children or be surrounded by coworkers and friends, and yet she could be the loneliest person around. Her sense of isolation is usually internal, and she may believe that if she were to articulate her feelings to anyone, she would be met with derision or even rebuke. "How can you be lonely," people would ask, "when you have such a wonderful husband and two beautiful children?" Despite the people around her, the reality of loneliness covers her like a shroud.

Sometimes people are lonely but don't even realize it. We can cover up our loneliness in so many ways: by throwing ourselves into the hustle and bustle of life, filling our houses with material possessions as we pursue dollar after dollar, or even busying ourselves with church work rather than kingdom work. But when it's all said and done, if we do not address the root of our loneliness, it will gnaw at our hearts from the time we lay down at night until we wake up in the morning.

The distraction of loneliness causes an *echo in the soul*, a reverberation of thoughts and questions that bounce around in your spirit, ultimately springing from a sense of emptiness: *Does anybody see me? Does anybody know what I'm going through? Does anybody understand? Does anybody really care?*

I have gone through times in my life when, even though I had loved ones surrounding and supporting me, I still struggled with a deep, profound loneliness. I don't know what *caused* it, but I do know that I *felt* it. This was not only true for me—many people who are lonely could not legitimately tell you why. For this reason I have come to believe that loneliness is an attack of the enemy upon the mind and spirit. He seeks to fatally distract you by instilling in you a sense of isolation and separation. You feel disconnected, disjointed, as though you don't quite fit in or belong. You even feel disconnected from the people closest to you—your husband, your children, your family and friends. And unless you become plugged back in and reconnected with other people, the fatal distraction of loneliness can overcome you.

Thank God that we have a High Priest who can sympathize with our times of loneliness. All of Jesus' disciples and friends abandoned Him in the hours before He faced the cross. But Jesus had these words to say about that time: "Behold, the hour cometh, yea, is now come, that ye shall be scattered, every man to his own, and shall leave me alone: *and yet I am not alone, because the Father is with me*" (John 16:32, emphasis added).

Jesus' words in this passage are so very simple yet so utterly profound. In them lies our answer to the potentially fatal distraction of loneliness: We are *never* alone, and there is no need to feel lonely, because God is with us!

Lonely heart, allow the loving hand of God to reach down into your mind, heart and spirit and drive out the feelings of isolation and disconnection that plague you. Open your eyes and see, really see, where you are and what you have as a child of God. Elevate your mind above your circumstances, above your surroundings and environment, and realize that a true sense of connection and completeness will never come from factors *outside you*; it can only come from within you. Stop seeking fulfillment and identity from external sources, especially from other people, for disappointment often causes retreat—and isolation and loneliness will soon follow. Denounce the fatal distraction of loneliness and seize the day! Embrace the will and plan of God for your life, and let your wholeness come from Him in whom there is no lack, only inexhaustible supply.

CHAPTER 11

Anger

S OLOMON, THE WISEST man—aside from Christ—to ever
live on the earth, had these words to say about a
woman who was continually angry: "It is better to
dwell in the wilderness, than with a contentious and an
angry woman" (Prov. 21:19). Remember, this advice was
coming from a man who himself had seven hundred wives
and three hundred concubines (1 Kings 11:3). Solomon
knew what he was talking about!

The dictionary defines *anger* as "a strong feeling of dis-
pleasure and usually of antagonism."[1] When someone is
antagonistic, they "*actively* express opposition or hostility."[2] The word *actively* in this definition implies that
anger is not something that can be easily hidden. Even
though we may be able to smile in each other's faces for a
time, if true anger is present, it will eventually manifest
itself one way or another.

Anger is a fatal distraction because of its exceptionally
destructive nature: If left unchecked, it can destroy not
only the person experiencing it, but also everyone in its
path.

Interestingly, the Latin origin of the word *anger* is actually *angere*, which means "to strangle."[3] A person under

the control of the fatal distraction of anger will attempt to crush and strangle the object of that anger, not necessarily in a literal sense (although that may occur!), but certainly in an emotional and spiritual sense. Anger is emotionally fatal, in that it strangles the positive outlook of the one who is bound by it and causes that person to look at life and other people through hostile, antagonistic eyes. Anger strangles any feelings of mercy—it is impossible for someone who is filled with anger to even desire to be merciful, much less extend mercy.

> If left unchecked, anger can destroy not only the person experiencing it, but also everyone in its path.

RIGHTEOUS ANGER

Interestingly, not all anger is bad. We are given some latitude in the Word of God: Ephesians 4:26 tells us to "be angry, and yet do not sin" (NAS).

When is anger a good and righteous emotion? Let me give you some examples. It angers me when women are exploited through pornography, or when innocent blood is shed through the horror of abortion. I feel righteous anger when I hear a news report of a child being abducted and molested, or of an elderly person being attacked and robbed. To not be angered by these things would be a sin, and to not feel anger when I myself am a victim of prejudice or unfair treatment would not be an expression of my natural, God-given emotions. But I am sinning because of my anger when I fail to effectively handle that anger in a spiritual, biblical way. To not give in to anger and sin, I must allow myself to be guided and controlled by the Holy Spirit and by the law of love, for love "is not easily provoked" (1 Cor. 13:5). I must maintain an active and working knowledge of the Word of God—I must hide the Word in my heart, that I might not sin against God. (See Psalm 119:11.)

Anger that is controlled by a sense of righteousness will never seek to hurt or destroy another, and the expression of that anger will not be made in an ungodly manner. If I walk in the Spirit, anger at the manifestation of the work of the enemy will cause me to pray rather than to gossip, to intercede rather than to judge and condemn. Anger expressed righteously will cause me to be angry at sin, yet love the sinner and desire his salvation.

ANGER WITHOUT REASON

While there are permissible reasons for and expressions of anger, the vast majority of the anger we experience is not justifiable. The fatal distraction of anger often manifests itself in unjustifiable ways and will always get us in trouble with God. In Matthew 5:22, Jesus said, "Whosoever is angry with his brother without a cause shall be in danger of the judgment." Anger is a dangerous business!

Sometimes we are angry with people when we have no justifiable reason to be. They may not have even bothered us or sinned against us, yet for some reason when we see them, we lash out against them. We find ourselves angry at them for the most inane and inexcusable reasons: because they're short, tall, light, dark, pretty, unattractive, overweight, underweight, old, young—you name it!

This type of anger is irrational and petty, and it arises primarily when we are actually angry and dissatisfied with ourselves. A woman who loves and is happy with herself has no need—and usually no time—to be angered by the real or imagined characteristics of someone else.

How I long for the day when women everywhere can celebrate one another instead of viewing each other as the enemy! The fatal distraction of anger promotes disunity, for how can I effectively work with you if I am angered by you? Women of God, let's stop being petty and catty, lashing out against one another for no good reason! Instead of resisting your sister's beauty or skills, celebrate them! Choose to compliment your sisters on their attributes or talents rather than being spiteful or even vicious. So often we think of men as the ones who hold us back, but no one can tear a woman apart like another woman! And I dare say that there are very few women, if any, who have not been either on the giving end or the receiving end of malevolent comments that stem from unjustifiable anger.

Why are so many women so angry today? Where have all these angry, hostile and antagonistic emotions come from? In addition to the anger that arises from dissatisfaction with one's self, fatal anger can arise within a woman who is angry with herself. Ultimately, a woman who is angry with herself has, for whatever reason, not forgiven herself. Think about it: A woman who has not forgiven herself for her own illegitimate pregnancy will usually be especially harsh or critical of unwed teenage mothers. If a woman is overweight and has not "forgiven" herself for her physical appearance, she will be defensive and easily offended by women who are "skinny." A person who is "forgiven much, loves much," and when we are able to forgive ourselves for our own indiscretions and shortcomings, we are not as easily tempted to strike out against others.

Just as not forgiving ourselves will cause us to be angry women, harboring unforgiveness toward others will also cause us to lash out in anger. And in addition to the sin of expressing hostile anger toward someone, if we refuse forgiveness to her, we cut off the flow of forgiveness that God would extend toward us. "For if ye forgive men their trespasses," Jesus said, "your heavenly Father will also forgive you: But if you forgive not men their trespasses, neither will your Father forgive your trespasses" (Matt. 6:14–15).

I know a woman who was passed over for a promotion in favor of a recently hired, less-qualified coworker. This woman was angry on so many different levels: She was angry with her supervisor for passing her over, angry with the coworker who "stole" the promotion, angry with new employees in general because, in her words, "they always get ahead not by *what* they know but *who* they know." She was even angry with herself for applying for the job in the first place! She was well on her way to being destroyed by the fatal distraction of anger, until she was finally able to forgive everyone involved, apply for another position and move on to enjoy a happy, productive life of her own.

Forgiveness and release can loosen the hold of unresolved anger, anger that has not yet been dealt with successfully. The woman who had been passed over finally realized that she had to bring some resolution to her anger. She understood that refusing to forgive the actions of her supervisor and coworker would continue to obstruct the flow of the Spirit in her own life. She had already suffered enough—she refused to extend the suffering by allowing what had happened to overshadow the rest of her life. Not only did God give her the strength to forgive and release the offending parties, but He also gave her the grace to do so, for it was not His desire to have the life of His daughter marred by the effects of anger.

It takes the grace of God to let go of anger and release forgiveness in such a heartbreaking situation, but it is possible, for we can "do everything through him [Christ] who gives [us] strength" (Phil. 4:13, NIV).

THE BALM OF FORGIVENESS

I recall an occasion when I was extremely angry with another individual. I felt that I had been "betrayed" by this person, and it was difficult for me to let go of the anger and animosity I felt. Every time I saw her, the feelings of betrayal and the subsequent anger would surface, to the point that it was hard for me to even look at her! I was actually nurturing my anger as if it were a baby. I repeatedly rehearsed the offense over and over, actually building up a resistance and opposition in my spirit toward that person! Throughout this time, the Holy Spirit continued to whisper the words of Ephesians 4:26–27 to my heart: "Be ye angry, and sin not: *let not the sun go down upon your wrath:* Neither give place to the devil" (emphasis added). Eventually I listened to the conviction in my spirit, and I resolved I would release not only the anger, but also the person with whom I was so angry.

But how?

Those words—"I released my anger"—seem so easy to say, but they are so hard to actually do! But I was determined to be free, so I decided that I would set aside seven days as a consecration period unto the Lord. I not only fasted from food, but I also turned off my television for seven days. In addition, I made sure that I did not cross paths with the person with whom I was angry for that seven-day period.

When seeking the Lord during this time about how not to "let the sun go down on my wrath" again—I had already seen quite a few sunsets!—I asked Him to give me an understanding of what those words really meant. The Lord gave me an illustration of how in my day-to-day life, I would prepare for bed. I would wash my face and brush my teeth. I would go to my closet, find an outfit and a pair of shoes for the next day, and lay them out as well. I would usually have all of these tasks done by a certain time every night so that I could get enough sleep.

> **Forgiveness and release can loosen the hold of unresolved anger.**

God showed me that just as I took steps to ensure that I was prepared for bed by a certain time, I should also make the necessary preparations to get rid of my anger by a certain time—in this case, before the sun went down! He showed me that I should do whatever it took—even if it meant calling the person to repent, working through the problem in an effort to resolve it, or praying and asking God for His grace to walk in love toward that person.

Whatever it took to let go of the anger, I needed to have it done before the sun went down! Needless to say, once the Lord made it so plain and so clear to me, it became much easier for me to follow through and obey Him in that area of my life.

"OUTRAGEOUS" ANGER

Proverbs 27:4 says, "Wrath is cruel, and anger is outrageous." Wrath, a more intense form of anger, depicts "a strong vengeful anger or indignation," or "retributory punishment for an offense or crime."[4] To get to the point of experiencing wrath, you have "stewed over" whatever has made you angry and allowed your emotions to run rampant. This happens when we fail to nip our angry, negative thoughts in the bud—right when they occur—and refuse to follow Paul's admonition to "[cast] down our imaginations" and to "[bring] into captivity every thought to the obedience of Christ" (2 Cor. 10:5).

Have you ever seen an angry, out-of-control woman when she has reached the "outrageous" state? No matter how physically beautiful she may ordinarily be, she is not at all beautiful at that moment, is she? What characterizes her? Usually a raised voice, flushed cheeks, heaving chest and a mind that is totally closed to reason. This is such an outrageous spectacle that it is said twice in the Book of Proverbs: "It is better to dwell in a corner of the housetop, than with a brawling woman in a wide house" (Prov. 21:9; 25:24).

What amazes me even more is that some women actually take pride in their ability to "raise Cain"— whether at home, in the workplace or even at church!

Their undisciplined releases of anger erroneously give them a feeling of power. They may even arrogantly boast, "I don't put up with anything!"

If this is your mentality, stop it at once! You are standing in opposition to the very Word of God. Having temper tantrums and "going off" on people do not mean you have mastered a situation—they only display that the situation has mastery over you. Consider the words of Scripture: "He that is slow to anger is better than the mighty; and he that ruleth his spirit than he that taketh a city" (Prov. 16:32).

Giving in to your anger rather than reining it in will cause you to commit foolish responses and actions. Do you disagree with me? Do you somehow think you are smart when you "blow your top?" Proverbs 14:17 says, "He that is soon angry dealeth foolishly," and Ecclesiastes 7:9 says, "Be not hasty in thy spirit to be angry: for anger resteth in the bosom of fools."

Indulging your anger makes you reactive instead of proactive. Rather than addressing a situation and anticipating future problems before it gets out of control, you explosively respond to whatever is confronting you. A woman usually has a fairly good idea of what "pushes her buttons," and one who is mature enough to exercise self-control will not allow her nose to get "out of joint" easily. Giving vent to one's anger and a lack of self-control go hand in hand, for "he that hath no rule over his own spirit is like a city that is broken down, and without walls" (Prov. 25:28).

Being prone to excessive anger is neither cute nor attractive; it only shows that you have problems in your own life. I urge you to identify quickly those broken areas in your life, and then ask God to help you rebuild those areas before the enemy tries to ensnare you even further. Jesus said that "when a strong man, fully armed, guards his own homestead, his possessions are undisturbed" (Luke 11:21, NAS). Spiritually, you must allow the Holy Spirit to be the "strong man" who guards your heart. When He braces the weakened areas in your life, specifically those areas that have caused you so much anger, then you will be able to guard the other areas of your life that the devil seeks to invade. You see, the enemy is not content with your just being angry at a coworker—he wants you to be angry with your boss, your husband, your children, even your pastor. But "the wrath of man worketh not the righteousness of God" (James 1:20).

> Stand in agreement with the Word of God and be that new creature. Refuse to allow your life to be characterized and ruled by anger.

Shore yourself up in repentance and prayer, and ask God to reveal to you exactly what it is that is making you angry. Don't make excuses and say, "I'm just standing up for myself," or "This is just my personality," for when you receive Christ, He makes all things new and you become a new creation (2 Cor. 5:17). Stand in agreement with the Word of God and be that new creature. Refuse to allow your life to be characterized and ruled by anger. And if you must be angry at something, be angry at the way anger is destroying your life and the life of those you love!

CHAPTER 12

Bitterness

THE STORY OF Job in the Old Testament has come to symbolize the plight of a person who has endured great pain, suffering and loss. But Job can be a great example for us of how to keep bitterness from laying a claim to our hearts. Not only did Job lose all of his possessions—his cattle and all of his wealth—but he also lost by violent death every one of his seven sons and three daughters. As if all that wasn't devastating enough, Job's health deteriorated until his entire body was covered with painful boils. Still, he did not sin by cursing God.

Despite his steadfast trust in the Lord, Job did go through a stage of questioning God as to the reason for the mishaps that had befallen him. When presenting these questions to God, he said, "Therefore I will not refrain my mouth; I will speak in the anguish of my spirit; I will complain in the bitterness of my soul" (Job 7:11). Job experienced feelings of bitterness because of the calamities that had befallen his life, but fortunately he was able to cope successfully with those feelings, and eventually there was a complete restoration of everything he had lost.

Something that is bitter is "distasteful or distressing to the mind, galling."[1] Bitterness is a feeling that is "marked by intensity and severity," one that expresses a feeling of "intense animosity, cynicism, or contempt."[2]

Someone whose life is characterized by the fatal distraction of bitterness usually experiences very little joy, for she is too focused upon the source of the bitterness to see many other good things occurring in her life. When you meet such people, their bitterness becomes readily apparent because their words and sentiments betray them. God tells us that a bitter attitude is not an acceptable way of life for His children: "Let all bitterness, and wrath, and anger, and clamour, and evil speaking, be put away from you, with all malice" (Eph. 4:31).

A bitter heart often manifests itself through comments or "jokes" that are actually veiled put-downs. These put-downs can be subtle, such as, "That outfit would be a knockout with different shoes." Or they can be more blatant, such as when someone says, "Those Capris are cute, but do you really think someone your size should wear them?"

A bitter woman will find it hard to say anything good about anybody, because her words will flow out of the abundance of her poisoned heart. When she makes a comment, others often think, *Where did that come from?* Be wary of bitter people, and be wary of being a bitter person yourself!

Sources of Bitterness

Unfortunately, one source of bitterness is people who embitter the lives of others, primarily because it makes them feel superior. They may be a boss or supervisor on the job, using their place of command to oppress others. This happened to the nation of Israel during their time of slavery. The Egyptians "made their lives bitter with hard bondage, in mortar, and in brick, and in all manner of service in the field: all their service, wherein they made them serve, was with rigour" (Exod. 1:14).

For a time, it seemed as if the people of God were trapped. They were slaves in the hands of Pharaoh, and on the surface there appeared to be no way out of their bondage. Perhaps our country's current economic woes and the deflated job market are giving you pause as well, causing you to feel that you are stuck in your

> Someone whose life is characterized by the fatal distraction of bitterness usually experiences very little joy.

unpleasant work environment. Take heart! Just as God raised up a deliverer so long ago, He will bring about deliverance for you as well. Don't allow yourself to despair, and by all means don't allow yourself to fall victim to the fatal distraction of bitterness. Use that oppressive situation as an opportunity to let the light of your salvation in Christ shine through. Don't hide your light under a "bushel" of resentment, but let it radiate and honor God in the process: "Let your light so shine before men," Jesus said, "that they may see your good works, and glorify your Father which is in heaven" (Matt. 5:16).

In time, God moved on behalf of His people, and Pharaoh said, "Rise up, and get you forth from among my people, both ye and the children of Israel; and go...take your flocks and your herds...be gone; and *bless me also*"

(Exod. 12:31–32, emphasis added). One way or another, you will also be able to magnify God for the deliverance you will experience in your workplace.

Sometimes we may feel bitterness against someone for the wrongs they have committed against us. Some of us could, at the drop of a hat, recite the name, address, telephone number and social security number of the person who has wronged us!

Let me share a modern-day parable to show what bitterness can do to you.

The Story of Chelsea and Valerie

Chelsea, a real estate agent, was having a difficult time overcoming deep-seated feelings of resentment against Valerie, her former best friend.

After years of trying to have a child, Chelsea and her husband became the proud adoptive parents of Corey, a happy, rambunctious, three-year-old boy. A stay-at-home mom, Valerie is the mother of two boys and a girl, aged nine, six and four respectively. A "seasoned" mother (and Corey's godmother), she often teased Chelsea about her tendency to be overprotective of Corey. Though Valerie had often encouraged Chelsea when she was depressed over her seeming inability to conceive, and consequently understood why Corey was so precious to her friend, she believed that Chelsea's constant "smothering" would eventually have an ill effect on her son. Chelsea, on the other hand, strongly believed that Valerie was a little too relaxed in her parenting and that she needed to be more diligent and watchful.

The four children were invited to a birthday party being held on the same day and time that Chelsea was scheduled to show an expensive property to a prospective buyer. Eager to do what she could to help her friend make the sale, Valerie offered to pick Corey up and then bring him back home after the party. Reluctantly, Chelsea agreed.

"I should have followed my first instinct," she says regretfully. "Though Valerie was my best friend and I loved her very much, I had never been comfortable with the way she handled her kids. To me, she let them fend for themselves. I admit that I watch Corey very carefully, but I'm his mother—I'm supposed to protect him and make sure his environment is a safe one. When Valerie made her offer, I hesitated, but I gave in. The party would only last a couple of hours, and I figured that with all the other mothers around, nothing major would happen."

Unfortunately, Chelsea was wrong. While playing outside, Corey had a head-on collision with one of the older children and had to be taken to the emergency room for stitches. Though the emergency room physician did a good job, Corey was left with a faint but permanent scar on his forehead. After getting over her initial hysteria, Chelsea was livid with Valerie.

"Every time I see Corey's scar, I get angry all over again," Chelsea says. "My child's *neck* could have been broken! I blame Valerie *totally* for the accident because she should have been watching him more closely! It's one thing to be lackadaisical with your own children, but when you volunteer to be responsible for someone else's child, there's no excuse for carelessness."

In addition to her anger, Chelsea started focusing on all of her friend's shortcomings and failures, and she eventually became bitter against Valerie. Fueled by the sight of Corey's scar, she began to obsess over the accident and brooded over what she would have done if he had been killed. She became so consumed by the "what ifs" that not only did she forget to appreciate all that was loving and good in Valerie—she also neglected to be grateful to God for the accident not being worse than it was!

Chelsea became extremely paranoid about her son's well-being—to the point of almost refusing to let him out of her sight. Her anger and bitterness at Valerie placed a great strain on their friendship, and her compulsive behavior toward her son began to affect her marriage. Even though she blamed Valerie for "traumatizing" her son and her, in actuality, Chelsea was allowing the fatal distraction of bitterness to undermine her peace of mind and her life.

Let God Turn Your Situation for Good

Just as Job's situation caused him to question God's purpose for his life, there may be incidents and misfortunes that cause us to wonder what God is doing, but we must continue to maintain our faith that nothing is allowed to enter our lives without first being permitted by God. For all the damage that he inflicted, the devil first had to go through God before he could attack Job, and even then, he remained under God's watchful supervision. (See Job 1:12.) Rest assured that God knows your situation. He is so attuned to you that "even the very hairs of your head are all numbered" (Luke 12:7).

If you feel that life has dealt you a bad hand, and even if there actually are persons who have done you wrong, begin to approach the events in your life with the same spirit of discernment that Joseph used. Despite being sold into slavery by his brothers, through a set of divinely orchestrated circumstances, he eventually became the prime minister of Egypt and was even

> **We must continue to maintain our faith that nothing is allowed to enter our lives without first being permitted by God.**

instrumental in saving his family from perishing in famine. When their father passed away, his brothers were worried and said to themselves, "Joseph will peradventure hate us, and will certainly requite us all the evil which we did unto him" (Gen. 50:15).

After all of the things that had happened, Joseph could have chosen to become "bitter," instead of "better," and sought revenge against his brothers. Fortunately, they did ask for his forgiveness: "Forgive, I pray thee now, the trespass of thy brethren, and their sin; for they did unto thee evil: and now, we pray thee, forgive the trespass of thy servants of the God of thy Father" (v. 17). They even took their repentance a step further: "And his brethren also went and fell down before his face; and they said, Behold, we be thy servants" (v. 18).

There are times in our walk with God that He will make our enemies our footstool, as Psalm 110:1 says, and we are presented with the opportunity to either get revenge, continue to be at enmity with them or forgive them in love.

Bitterness could have driven Joseph to focus upon the horrible crime that had been committed against him. Instead of seeing the divine providence of God at work, the fatal distraction of bitterness could have caused Joseph to spurn his brothers' request for forgiveness and refuse to grant it. He could have had them sold into slavery, imprisoned them or even put them to death. But instead he comforted and consoled his brothers, and graciously said, "Fear not: for am I in the place of God?" (Gen. 50:19).

> **When you refuse to forgive, you are actually standing in the place of God!**

It is helpful to keep in mind that footstools are used to take us to another level. When you utilize a footstool, it is always to take a step up—to go higher! You don't need a footstool unless you are changing levels, so rejoice! Thank God for the "footstools"!

We must be very, very careful that when people come to us asking for forgiveness, we remember these words of Jesus:

> Take heed to yourselves: If thy brother trespass against thee, rebuke him; and if he repent, *forgive him.* And if he trespass against thee seven times in a day, and seven times in a day turn again to thee, saying, I repent; *thou shalt forgive him.*
> —LUKE 17:3–4, EMPHASIS ADDED

Nowhere in this passage did Jesus instruct us to "analyze" their repentance, have us determine if they are "really sorry" or question whether they understand what they did to us. Their sincerity should not be your concern; what should be your concern is your response, for that is what you will be held accountable for.

When you refuse to forgive, and instead choose to hold on to your unforgiveness and bitterness, you are actually standing in the place of God! Could any of us repay the debt of sin that we owed to God? Would not all of us have been lost forever but for the redemptive work of Christ on the cross and the availability of His freely offered salvation? Paul made this argument in Romans 3:23–27:

> For all have sinned, and come short of the glory of God; being justified freely by his grace through the redemption that is in Christ Jesus: Whom God hath set forth to be a propitiation through faith in his blood, to declare his righteousness for the remission of sins that are past, through the forbearance of God; to declare, I say, at this time his righteousness: that he might be just, and the justifier of him which believeth in Jesus. Where is boasting then? It is excluded. By what law? Of works? Nay: but by the law of faith.

Since you wronged God and had to be forgiven by Him, and the person who wronged you had to be forgiven by God, how is it, then, that you have the right to hold them in bitterness and unforgiveness?

Joseph went on to say, "But as for you, ye thought evil against me; but God meant it unto good, to bring to pass, as it is this day, to save much people alive" (Gen. 50:20). Joseph perfectly typified Christ, who, "while we were yet sinners…died for the ungodly" (Rom. 5:8, 6). No matter what has happened to you, my sister, no matter how many wrongs have been done to you, the love and grace of God are readily available to help you let go of the bitterness in your heart and give you the ability to release the persons who wronged you.

Ask God to give you the spiritual wisdom and discernment He gave Joseph and to permit you to see the good He is bringing out of your situation. If you do this, you will become better, not bitter, and you will walk in the blessings God has custom-designed just for you!

CHAPTER 13

Hurt and Brokenness

S EVERAL YEARS AGO Whitney Houston popularized the words to a song titled, "Where Do Broken Hearts Go?" At that time, it topped the charts and was on the lips of many women in America.

Why did it become so popular? The talent of Whitney Houston notwithstanding, the words to the song stand out because they address a fatal distraction to which most women can relate: hurt and brokenness. According to the dictionary, to hurt means to "cause emotional pain or anguish; offend or be detrimental to."[1] When we hurt, we "suffer pain or grief, are in need, or have been caused damage or distress."[2]

Many women today are literally the "walking wounded." Millions go about their daily activities, all the while keeping up the façade that everything is all right in their world. But on the inside they are hurt, wounded and broken.

When these women come to know Jesus Christ in His fullness and become a part of the church, many of them soon develop an "everything's-going-to-be-all-right" mentality. In one sense, everything was all right because their sins had been washed away, but in another sense, most of them soon experienced a frightening reality check—they learned that coming into God's kingdom did not guarantee a "bed of ease." Becoming a Christian did not safeguard them from continued hurt and brokenness.

All of us have made that reality check at some point in our Christian walk, when we discovered that being saved does not exempt us from unfair treatment and continued troubles, trials or afflictions. Having Jesus in your heart doesn't necessarily mean that your heart will never again be broken!

Have you ever endured the pain of a broken heart? When something is broken, it is "violently separated into parts, shattered or damaged."[3] Now we understand that the heart is so much more than just the muscular organ in our chest that pumps blood throughout our body. In a different sense, our heart refers to the center of all of our emotions and affections. Just as the mind is our intellectual component, the heart is our emotional core.

BROKEN RELATIONSHIPS WITH MEN

Almost all of us have experienced a broken heart at one time or another. And for most of us, the primary cause for such pain is disappointment in unsatisfactory, lost or broken relationships. Earlier we considered the life of Leah—she was married to Jacob and loved him very much, but she loved a man who never did and never would love her in return. Instead, he was in love with her sister, Rachel, so much so that he was willing to work a total of fourteen years for her hand in marriage. Imagine Leah's humiliation when Jacob discovered her, not Rachel, in his marriage bed, and then he agreed to work seven more years to still be able to marry her sister! Even after Leah bore children for Jacob, she was never able to win his love.

Another example in the Bible of a woman who suffered from the pain of a broken relationship was Michal, the wife of David. She was used as a pawn by her father, Saul, who offered her to David as a means of spying on him and his interests. Michal was separated from her husband in the early months of her marriage; since he was on the run from her father, the quality time that should have gone to her went to other wives.

> **Just as the mind is our intellectual component, the heart is our emotional core.**

What emotions did Michal experience during this time? Michal loved David so much that even King Saul, her father, knew it and was angered by it (1 Sam. 18:28). She loved David so much that she went so far as to circumvent her father's plan to murder him by helping David to escape. (See 1 Samuel 19:12–17.)

Even though her assistance had ensured David's freedom, it also essentially took David away from her. He had escaped Saul, but he was still on the run, and he eventually took two other wives during this time: the beautiful Abigail, the widow of Nabal, and Ahinoham of Jezreel. And eventually Michal was given as a wife to another man: "But Saul had given Michal his daughter, David's wife, to Phalti to son of Laish, which was of Gallim" (1 Sam. 25:44).

First, Michal was unable to enjoy her marriage to the man she loved, and then, to add insult to injury, she was given in marriage to another! I can only imagine the hurt and disappointment she felt, knowing that her culture would allow David to marry other wives and that her father's hatred of David had caused her to be given to someone else. Evidently the fatal distraction of bitterness got the best of her, for when David returned in triumph, she was critical of him rather than joyful at his return. (See 2 Samuel 6:16, 20.)

There are further examples of brokenhearted women in the New Testament: the woman at the well who had five husbands, the woman caught in the act of adultery and the woman who was so broken by her sinful life that she washed Jesus' feet with the hairs of her head. All of us can likely identify with at least one of the women I have mentioned.

REJECTION

Just about everyone can identify with a broken heart, whether they are a saint or a sinner. Like rejection, hurt and brokenness are fatal distractions that are accompanied by pain—emotional pain that can become so real that it actually feels like physical pain. Pain is defined as "acute mental or emotional distress or suffering; grief."[4] While physical pain is certainly a force to be reckoned with, emotional pain is generally far, far worse. Emotional pain cuts deeply into your soul and spirit, leaving you maimed and numb.

I can recall a time when I was suffering from the grief and pain caused by the untimely loss of my husband. The pain of that loss caused me to retreat from life. But for the grace and supernatural intervention of God, I would have succumbed to this fatal distraction and lived a life that was consumed by grief. But with time, I healed and was able to embrace life again, to the point that I was ready to share my heart again in love. Having already deeply loved one man, I was more prone to invest all of my heart into what became a promising relationship with another respectable, good-looking man. Although he lived in another city, we corresponded often and took every opportunity to spend quality time together. Things seemed to be going very well; my newfound love and I were extremely compatible, we shared similar spiritual views and greatly enjoyed one another's company. One evening at the close of a particularly delightful long-distance conversation, he told me he had an errand to run and would call me later. As it turned out, the "later" lasted two years! For two years I did not hear from him—not by phone call, letter or message. It was as if he had vanished from the face of the earth, dropping me in the process.

While physical pain is certainly a force to be reckoned with, emotional pain is generally far, far worse.

Words cannot express the anguish and pain I experienced during those two years! Initially, I thought he had just gotten busy; he had a demanding job and sometimes worked long, grueling hours. But as time went by and my calls went unreturned, my nonchalance turned to alarm, and after discovering that he was indeed alive and well, my alarm turned into anger and finally into a deep, abiding hurt.

Questions flooded my mind: Why had he stopped calling? Why had he simply dropped me? He had told me that he loved me! Instead of embarking on a life filled with love and promise, I had suffered yet another excruciatingly painful loss. My every waking moment was filled with pain: the pain of his rejection, the pain of not knowing why, the pain of unrequited love, the pain of being alone, the pain of self-doubt, insecurity and fear.

During those two years, I got up every day and went to my job, had lunch with my coworkers and even got great job reviews. I visited my mother, went on outings with my sisters, laughed with my brothers and played with my nieces and nephews. I kept going to church and even presided over the missionary board! But all of this work, all of this living, all of this ministry was masked by a cloak of pain.

Eventually I reached a point where I could not take the pain of another loss any longer, and I decided that I no longer wanted to live. I drove to a nearby lake, parked my car at the water's edge and looked around one last time before I was to drive in. But when I reached to put my car in gear, I was startled by the voice of a man yelling, "Hey! What are you doing?" Not seeing anyone and frightened out of my wits, I put my car in reverse and hastily drove away. But as I drove back home, trembling and sobbing, the Holy Spirit spoke to my wearied and troubled mind:

> When peace, like a river, attendeth my way,
> When sorrows like sea billows roll;
> Whatever my lot, thou hast taught me to say,
> It is well, it is well with my soul.[5]

These powerful words from a well-known hymn broke my almost-fatal distraction, and I was able to go on to a renewed life, healed and whole.

BROKEN RELATIONSHIPS WITH OTHER WOMEN

We can experience hurt and brokenness in relationships both with men and with other women. Hagar was a woman who experienced heartache in both arenas. As a servant to Sarah, her life was not her own, and it was eventually totally disrupted by the circumstances in which she found herself. Sarah's desire to have a child became so strong that she became willing to do whatever it took— including having her husband, Abraham, impregnate her handmaiden. A hapless pawn, Hagar had no choice but to obey her mistress and serve as an intermediary through which a baby might be born.

Forced to have a sexual relationship with the husband of her boss, so to speak, Hagar was impregnated by Abraham and bore a child. At some point the injustice of the situation and the complete disregard by Sarah of Hagar's personal feelings caused her to respond to Sarah with contempt. This resentment boiled over, and finally Hagar could not keep herself from showing her disdain.

Sarah, overcome with jealousy at Hagar's pregnancy and possible remorse at her ill-conceived plan, began to assert a "high-and-mighty" attitude toward Hagar, and the Bible says that Sarah "dealt hardly with her" (Gen. 16:6). Sarah was responding negatively to Hagar because of the hurt she felt at being barren! Can you imagine what the atmosphere in that home must have been like?

Unable to deal with Sarah's harsh treatment, Hagar finally fled the situation.

Many women today follow Hagar's example: Although they may not be at liberty to physically remove themselves from the painful situation, they "run away" in other ways: through overeating (or undereating), impulse shopping, excessive sleep, constant television watching, prescription painkillers or antidepressants, or other self-destructive behaviors.

Hagar ran away physically, but God met her in the midst of her flight and gave her reassurance and hope. And even though He instructed her to return to Sarah and submit to her, He also consoled her by revealing her son's name and future. The Lord reassured her that He had heard her cries and seen her affliction (Gen. 16:11). Her future was uncertain—she didn't know what she would face from Sarah upon her return—but Hagar rested securely in the knowledge that God was with her and was watching over her and her child (v. 13).

We are not told what coping mechanisms she used, but we do know that Hagar and her son, Ishmael, lived in Abraham's household for at least another thirteen years. I wonder if Hagar and Sarah ever became friends; there would forever be a rivalry not only between the two of them, but between their sons as well.

In addition to broken relationships, a broken heart is something with which just about everybody can identify, whether they are a saint or a sinner. As I pondered the fatal distraction of hurt, I thought about the women I have counseled with down through the years, women who were in various stages of dealing with their pain. I also thought about the different coping mechanisms I saw them use to deal with that pain. You see, like rejection, hurt and brokenness are fatal distractions that are accompanied by pain—an emotional pain so real as to actually feel like physical pain. Indeed, in large part, I believe that coping with the pain that comes with hurt is what makes the distraction so fatal!

As hard as it is to live under a façade, it is even harder to live under a façade that is characterized by pain. As I stated earlier in this chapter, pain is defined as "acute mental or emotional distress or suffering, grief."[6] While physical pain is a force to be reckoned with in and of itself, to me, emotional pain is far, far worse. Emotional pain cuts deeply into your soul and spirit, leaving you maimed and eventually numb. You go through the motions of life and even of ministry—working, taking care of your family, going to church and even preaching to and teaching others—but your pain is as constant and abiding as your right hand, and it doesn't ever seem to be alleviated or to go away. Sometimes the emotional pain and hurt are so severe that while you may not come to the point of actually taking your own life, you may come to the point of desiring that your life be taken. An impossible state of mind for a saint to be in, you say? Well, consider the prophet Elijah, who boldly confronted and attacked apostasy and idolatry, but who was so wearied and overwhelmed by the wickedness and hatred of Jezebel that he "requested for himself that he might die; and said, It is enough; now, O LORD, take away my life; for I am not better than my fathers" (1 Kings 19:4).

My friend Michelle tells me of a time when she deeply

hurt a friend of hers. A pastor's wife, she already had a circle of a few close friends and was not inclined to let anyone else in on more than just an "acquaintance" level. But she and a new member of the church named Le'Nora hit it off immediately. They discovered they had a lot in common, and they enjoyed laughing, talking and spending time together. Unfortunately, however, Michelle's already-established circle of friends became jealous, and one of them in particular warned her to "watch what you say to Le'Nora!" The friend seemed to think that this "new" person could not be trusted, that she had not been "proven" as Michelle's other, more long-term friends had been.

Michelle initially brushed the comments off. She was not getting the same "vibe" that her established friend said she was getting, so she did not think much of it. But when a much-publicized crisis in her family developed, in an effort to protect her husband's privacy, Michelle decided to not mention anything concerning the situation to her friends. When

Emotional pain cuts deeply into your soul and spirit, leaving you maimed and eventually numb.

Le'Nora made a casual reference about the crisis, the warning that Michelle had been given about Le'Nora came flooding back. Aware that she had not discussed the situation with her new friend and wondering where Le'Nora had gotten her "information," she decided to withdraw from Le'Nora's company to protect herself.

Michelle never gave Le'Nora a reason for her sudden coolness; she simply became suddenly "very busy" with other obligations. Le'Nora, of course, picked up on what was happening—that she was being dropped—and she became deeply wounded by the break in their relationship.

Several years went by, and eventually Michelle and Le'Nora reconnected and resumed their friendship. The family crisis long over, Michelle finally explained to her friend why she had so abruptly cut her off.

"I was extremely embarrassed," she says, "but I had to tell her what had happened. Protecting my husband and my family had been my first priority, and I ended up second-guessing my trust in her. Of course, what I should have done was talk to her about the problem, but instead, I panicked and almost destroyed what has become an endearing and lasting friendship. Le'Nora has gone the distance with me through the 'thick and thin' of life. Those other friends? We don't even communicate anymore!"

LOST OPPORTUNITIES

Just as broken relationships cause us pain, we can also experience the fatal distraction of hurt because of lost opportunities. We think about what we could have done, what we should have done, but did not do. If we could only turn back the clock and do it all over again, we would do things so differently!

Such was the case with Esau, who paid dearly for one lapse in judgment. Hebrews 12:16–17 tells us that "for one morsel of meat [he] sold his birthright…Afterward, when he would have inherited the blessing, he was rejected: for he found no place of repentance, though he sought it carefully with tears."

Can you identify with Esau's broken heart? Are you still paying for wrong choices that you have made, still brokenhearted because of lost opportunities? These lost opportunities not only fill us with regret and the pain of past mistakes, but also we often cannot find the grace to forgive ourselves.

I am reminded of how some years ago, I deeply hurt someone, in more than just one way. This person had entrusted me with her car, and while it was in my possession I wrecked it. She had no car insurance, and I had no money. When I returned it to her in such a damaged condition, it fell upon her to get it repaired since it was her only means of transportation. I was genuinely sorry for what had happened, but at the time sorry did not mean much. It certainly didn't pay for the damage I had so carelessly caused.

Every time I saw her, I was flooded with feelings of shame. She was gracious enough to genuinely forgive me, but it took a much longer time for me to let go of the hurt and embarrassment I felt as a result of that situation. I had to learn to forgive myself, and now when I see her, we laugh about the time I "tore up both her car and her bank account!"

HEALING THE PAIN

There are things we must do to put our lives back together and begin to heal the pain. After spending two years in excruciating pain over my lost love, God gave me steps to use to regain my emotional health. First, I made sure that I indulged in no idle time. Then I took the Word of God and literally saturated myself in it, spending all of my free time pouring over the pages of Scripture. I knew that the Word had healing and cleansing power, so I did my best to "bathe" and "anoint" myself in it every day.

In addition to filling myself with the Word, I began to develop new levels of praising God. Although the Lord had broken the power that the pain of my failed relationships had over me, I wanted to keep it from returning. Whenever thoughts of the man who spurned me would enter my mind—and they certainly did come—I took that moment as an opportunity to praise God, even if nothing more than saying, "Lord, I love You," or, "Lord, I adore You." I had memorized many of the psalms, and I began to offer these words to the Lord. I spoke them aloud when I was alone and repeated them in my mind while at work.

I changed my focus from pain to praise. By doing that, I was able to get a true, strong definition of who God really is, and as I meditated upon His attributes, I was filled with a sense of awe and appreciation. Even though His attributes seemed so contrary to what He had permitted to occur in my life, I still knew that the Word of God was true, that no matter what had happened to me, it did not negate the fact that He is still loving, holy, pure, faithful and just.

Finally, I had to make a conscious decision to extend the love of God toward my former boyfriend. I had to choose to love him, for in my flesh it was so easy to feel hatred. I know, what a revealing admission! I have to be honest enough to admit that my depth of pain literally made me want to hate him, but thankfully, I recognized the fact that I had a choice in the matter. I could forever nurse a grudge against the man who had so wounded me, or I could choose to go on loving him—not with romantic love, but with the agape love of God.

I learned that life is usually not as bad as we imagine it to be. My ex and I eventually made contact, and although we have remained friends, I have gone on to a life lived outside of his shadow—emotionally stronger, healthier and independent. The grace of God can and will bring the dawning of a new day: "Weeping may endure for a night, but joy comes in the morning" (Ps. 30:5, NKJV).

WHERE DO BROKEN HEARTS GO?

When emotional pain attaches itself to your innermost being, so much of your strength is spent coping and dealing with the hurt that you have no energy left to utilize the power of God that is able to deliver you. In my case, it took the divine intervention of God to bring about my rescue; for others, it takes the prayers and intercession of friends and loved ones in order for the chains of this fatal distraction to be broken.

If you are reading this and are in the throes of this or any type of hurt, take courage; know that there is a place for your hurting and broken heart to go—the arms of your loving heavenly Father. David declared in Psalm 51:17, "The sacrifices of God are a broken spirit: a broken and contrite heart, O God, thou wilt not despise." Daughter of Zion,

Where do hurt and broken hearts go? I'll tell you where they should go—to the Rock.

know that God does not despise your hurt and brokenness. Just as He saw the hurt and affliction of Hagar and spoke words of comfort to her, He sees you and desires to speak to you as well. Open your heart and spirit, and let the consolation of God wash away your hurt. Let Him speak the immortal words of that hymn to you: "It is well with your soul!"

Where do hurt and broken hearts go? I'll tell you where they should go—to the Rock. David said, "From the end of the earth will I cry unto thee, when my heart is overwhelmed: lead me to the rock that is higher than I" (Ps. 61:2). Go to the Rock that is our Lord, and find healing for your hurt and restoration for your brokenness.

CHAPTER 14

Fear

S OMEONE HAD BROKEN into my house.

At least that's what I thought when I arrived home from a long trip and saw my back door wide open. After the police arrived and we determined that nothing had been stolen, it seemed that the burglars had been foiled in their attempt.

The detective assigned to my case pointed out the footprints in the back yard and the clothes hanger the burglars had used to jimmy the lock, and then he spoke the fateful words, "So you see, they're probably going to come back." With that, he advised me to lock all of my doors, leave a light or two on and keep the phone directly beside my bed for the night. And then he left!

By that point I had gone from a state of relative calm to pronounced panic! I went on to bed, taking the precautions the police had advised, but I could not sleep. Every few minutes, I investigated the slightest noise—both real and imagined. Needless to say, I became pretty tired pretty fast.

Finally, I began to pray, "Lord, You said that You have not given me the spirit of fear. I know that You who keep Israel neither slumbers nor sleeps, but I need to! Please come into this room and speak to my spirit so that I can get some rest."

The Holy Spirit spoke to me as clear as a bell: "You have everything that you need on the inside of you. All the policeman did was speak what he knew to speak—and that's what you must do as well! Walk through your house and begin to speak forth My Word."

So that's what I did. I began to walk through the rooms of my house and quote the Scriptures: "Yea, though I walk through the valley of the shadow of death, I will fear no evil, for Thou art with me." I anointed the doorposts with oil, declaring, "Thou anointest my head with oil, my cup runneth over. Surely goodness and mercy shall follow me all the days of my life, and I will rest forever in the house of the Lord." I began to quote Psalm 27 aloud:

> **In the arsenal of fatal distractions, fear is one of the "big guns"!**

> The LORD is my light and my salvation; whom shall I fear? The LORD is the strength of my life; of whom shall I be afraid? When the wicked, even mine enemies and my foes, came upon me to eat up my flesh, they stumbled and fell. Though an host should encamp against me, my heart shall not fear: though war should rise against me, in this will I be confident.
>
> One thing have I desired of the LORD, that will I seek after; that I may dwell in the house of the LORD all the days of my life, to behold the beauty of the LORD, and to inquire in his temple. For in the time of trouble he shall hide me in his pavilion: in the secret of his tabernacle shall he hide me; he shall set me up upon a rock.

And now shall mine head be lifted up above mine enemies round about me: therefore will I offer in his tabernacle sacrifices of joy; I will sing, yea, I will sing praises unto the LORD. Hear, O LORD, when I cry with my voice: have mercy also upon me, and answer me. When thou saidst, Seek ye my face; my heart said unto thee, Thy face, LORD, will I seek. Hide not thy face far from me; put not thy servant away in anger: thou hast been my help; leave me not, neither forsake me, O God of my salvation.

When my father and my mother forsake me, then the LORD will take me up. Teach me thy way, O LORD, and lead me in a plain path, because of mine enemies. Deliver me not over unto the will of mine enemies: for false witnesses are risen up against me, and such as breathe out cruelty.

I had fainted, unless I had believed to see the goodness of the LORD in the land of the living. Wait on the LORD: be of good courage, and he shall strengthen thine heart: wait, I say, on the LORD.

And then I went back to bed and got a good night's sleep!

In the arsenal of fatal distractions, fear is one of the "big guns"! The word *fear* means "to be afraid of, to expect with alarm."[1] While being afraid often suggests weakness or cowardice, and in essence means "to be filled with fear or apprehension," fear itself has a greater grip and power.[2] Jesus foretold a time when fear would be commonplace: "And there shall be…upon the earth distress of nations, with perplexity…men's hearts failing them for fear" (Luke 21:25–26).

FATAL DISTRACTIONS

To a certain extent, that time is now, for fear is widespread in both the world and the church. The fatal distraction of fear hinders, cripples and even halts our efforts to fulfill the purposes of God. Fear is paralyzing; when we focus on our fear instead of exercising our faith, we are like the proverbial deer in the headlights of an oncoming car—death is swiftly heading our way, but we are too frozen with fear to move to safety.

It is important to identify the source of fear, because it certainly does not come from God! The Word says, "God hath not given us the spirit of fear; but of power, and of love, and of a sound mind" (2 Tim. 1:7). According to 1 John 4:18, "fear hath torment," and it should go without saying that God does not capriciously torment His people! Fear, in fact, comes from the pit of hell, and we do not have to allow it in our lives.

Why, then, does fear run rampant in the body of Christ? With an omniscient, omnipresent and omnipotent God as our Father, why are we so fearful? Faith and fear are in antithesis to each other; whichever is stronger in a person's heart will cancel the other out. We cannot be victorious, overcoming believers if we are too fearful to take God at His Word. The Spirit of God may be telling us to "launch out into the deep, and let down your nets for a catch," as He told Peter in Luke 5:4, but fear can prevent us from even setting foot in the boat!

When the angel Gabriel appeared to Mary to inform her that the Messiah would come through her, his first words were, "Fear not, Mary: for thou hast found favour with God" (Luke 1:30). Mary responded in faith, not fear, and witnessed the divine fulfillment of her appointed destiny.

Even her betrothed husband, Joseph, heeded the angel's exhortation, "*Fear not* to take unto thee Mary thy wife: for that which is conceived in her is of the Holy Ghost" (Matt. 1:20, emphasis added). Mary and Joseph banished the fear they certainly felt, and as a result our Lord and Savior was able to come to the earth.

FEAR OF THE FUTURE

The fatal distraction of fear can enter our lives when we become apprehensive of the future. Women are especially susceptible to this type of fear because we crave stability and security. Marriage counselors agree that the number-one problem in marriages is not incompatibility or even infidelity; rather, the greatest problems arise from financial stress. In this time of economic instability, it can be easy to fall victim to fear of our future financial stability, and such fear can wreak havoc in our family relationships. In the Sermon on the Mount, Jesus said that we should take no thought for our lives; He was telling us not to have fear about the material aspects of our lives. God provides for the flowers of the earth and the birds of the air. How much more will He care for us? (See Matthew 6:25–34.)

Fear can thrive in our hearts when we do not focus upon the Giver of life and the promises contained in His Word. Though terrible circumstances may arise and adverse situations may come, we must not yield to fear; instead, we are to trust our God and respond to the problem in faith. The writer of Hebrews told of the response of Moses' parents to a frightening situation: "By faith Moses, when he was born, was hid three months of his parents, because they saw he was a proper child; and they were not afraid of the king's commandment" (Heb. 11:23). Moses' parents refused to give more credence to the commandment of Pharaoh than they did to the commandments of God.

When fear is allowed to maintain a stronghold in our lives, it is because we are putting more faith in the tangible than the intangible and more attention upon the problem than on the Problem Solver. Paul said, "For our light affliction, which is but for a moment, worketh for us a far more exceeding and eternal weight of glory" (2 Cor. 4:17). But this glory is only worked for us "while we look not at the things which are seen, but at the things which are not seen." Paul goes on to tell us why we should do this: "For the things which are seen are *temporal*, but the things which are not seen are *eternal*" (v. 18, emphasis added).

Although there are many tangible things that would try to overcome our hearts with fear, these things are not actually a threat to us! I heard a speaker once ascribe these words to the acronym of fear: "False Evidence Appearing Real." Ultimately, the things that we fear are in God's hands; they are "false evidence" that there is a problem that cannot be handled—false because God is totally in control of the situation!

THE FEAR OF MEN

The fatal distraction of fear can also rear its ugly head through a fear of what other people will think, which can prevent you from carrying out your God-given assignments.

Just think, if Peter and the other apostles had been afraid of what the Jews thought, they never would have preached the gospel, especially to the Gentiles! Instead, they proclaimed the name of Jesus boldly, even though they were imprisoned for their faith. When questioned about their "illegal" activity, Peter answered boldly that their authority came from Jesus Christ. When commanded "not to speak at all nor teach in the name of Jesus," Peter and John cast caution (and fear) to the wind, and declared, "Whether it be right in the sight of God to hearken unto you more than unto God, judge ye. For we cannot but speak the things which we have seen and heard" (Acts 4:18–20).

When fear is allowed to maintain a stronghold in our lives, it is because we are putting more faith in the tangible than the intangible and more attention upon the problem than on the Problem Solver.

I must add that after they were released, Peter and John went back to the church and reported everything that had been said and done. Instead of caving in to fear, the entire church lifted up their voices to God in prayer: "Now, Lord, behold their threatenings: and grant unto thy servants, that with all boldness they may speak thy word" (v. 29). They did not allow the fatal distraction of fear to even take root—they immediately turned to God, the Source of their courage and strength.

Only God knows how many messages have not been preached or delivered, how many words of wisdom and words of knowledge not imparted, how many ministries not begun, songs not sung, mission trips not taken, churches not opened or prayers not prayed (or answered!) because of fear! God alone knows how many inventions are lying dormant, how many doors to new businesses stand unopened, how many books are unwritten, how many people have literally missed their calling—all because of the fear of man!

When it comes to the area of ministry, the Lord takes the matter of fear very seriously. Jesus told us to "fear not them which kill the body, but are not able to kill the soul: but rather fear him which is able to destroy both soul and body in hell" (Matt. 10:28). In the Book of Luke, He stated it this way: "But I will forewarn you whom ye shall fear: Fear him, which after he hath killed hath power to cast into hell; yea, I say unto you, Fear him" (Luke 12:5).

CONQUERING FEAR

God spoke to Jeremiah at the beginning of his prophetic ministry: "Say not, I am a child: for thou shalt go to all that I shall send thee, and whatsoever I command thee thou shalt speak. Be not afraid of their faces: for I am with thee to deliver thee, saith the LORD" (Jer. 1:7–8). God was so serious about Jeremiah's not yielding to the fear of man that He told him, "Speak unto them all that I command thee: be not dismayed at their faces, lest I confound thee before them" (v. 17).

How can we vanquish the fatal distraction of fear? When King Jehoshaphat and his nation were facing the prospect of annihilation by warring kings and their armies, God spoke to him: "Be not afraid nor dismayed by reason of this great multitude; for the battle is not yours, but God's" (2 Chron. 20:15). Not only did God give Jehoshaphat the assurance of victory, but He also gave him a battle plan by which to accomplish the success. The plan did not include swords or spears, because He told them, "Ye shall not need to fight in this battle: set yourselves, stand ye still, and see the salvation of the LORD with you, O Judah and Jerusalem: *fear not, nor be dismayed*; to morrow go out against them: for the LORD will be with you" (v. 17, emphasis added).

> **What defeats the fatal distraction of fear? Praise!**

What defeats the fatal distraction of fear? Praise! There is no way you can truly praise God from your heart and at the same time be gripped by fear. Praising God—extolling and magnifying His name, lifting Him up—takes you out of a carnal battleground and into a spiritual arena. Praise takes your mind off of your limitations, your inability, your frailty and your weakness, and it places it where it belongs instead: upon the immeasurable ability and unlimited power of Almighty God!

When I am confronted with fear, I say as David said: "What time I am afraid, I will trust in thee" (Ps. 56:3). David acknowledged that there were times when he was fearful, but he made a commitment to trust God during those times.

Go ahead, admit your fear—don't be foolish and pretend that you don't have it. Acknowledge it to God, but then confront it head-on through the authority of God's Word! Cast fear away with unrestrained praise. Recognize that fear is another fatal distraction in the enemy's bag of tricks, and let him know that you are not buying! Your life will not be destroyed by fear, you will fulfill your divine purpose and destiny, and the glory of God will be manifested in your life! Praise God!

CHAPTER 15

Rejection

COME HERE, JOYCE. I have to give you a ticket for free lunch," the teacher announced. Feeling more than a little self-conscious and humiliated by her tone, I approached her desk with trepidation, silently praying that my other classmates could not hear her words.

"Your parents have enrolled you in the Title 21 Lunch Program," she said coldly. "That means you get free lunches, and they don't have to pay for it. I'll be giving you a ticket every week."

I nodded and took the ticket, wishing the floor would open up and swallow me. I started to turn away and go back to my seat, but her unfriendly brown eyes bored into mine. "You'll never amount to anything," she said with disgust. "You'll never get out of the projects. You'll always be one of those people with your hand out, looking for a free ride."

I could only stare silently, frozen by the venom in her voice. She wasn't finished. She took a deep breath and then shifted into high gear, her chest heaving with the hatred in her tone. For what seemed like an eternity, I was treated to a tirade about the irresponsibility of families from the projects, the rampant out-of-wedlock pregnancies, divorces, dropouts, alcoholism and drug abuse. When she was finally finished, she looked at me with disdain and said, "You can go now." She went back to the papers on her desk without giving me another glance. Pretending that I did not see the derisive glances of my classmates, I slunk back to my seat, my heart crushed inside of me. I had been dismissed—not just for that day, but as far as my teacher was concerned, for the rest of my life—even though I was only eight years old.

Unfortunately, I had come face to face with the ugly reality of rejection for the first time. I had been officially labeled—from then on I was a "project kid." Project kids were never selected first for games, and they never got a chance to stand first in any line. Not only did their fellow classmates reject them, but the teachers did as well. They were never chosen to lead the pledge of allegiance or say the morning prayer. Project kids never got the lead in school plays—they "couldn't afford the costumes." Unless they happened to be extremely good in sports, they were essentially considered a nonentity.

DEFINING REJECTION

When someone rejects something, he refuses to accept the object of his rejection—in whatever form that may take. Rejection usually involves a "discarding of someone or something as useless or unsatisfactory," or "casting out or cutting off of the object of rejection."[1]

We all learn to express rejection at an early age. Consider the six-month-old who can't stand the green beans in the jar of baby food: He wrinkles his nose and immediately pushes the spoon—and the green beans—right out of his mouth! Or the youngster entering his "terrible twos" who rejects the idea of taking a nap and screams out a resounding "No!" at the mere suggestion. Or the five-year-old girl who refuses to wear her blue shoes with her denim outfit; she insists on wearing the pink ones.

We all decide who and what we like and do not like, and we make no bones about telling others about our selections—and rejections. Although this may seem "cute" when we are little, eventually we become old enough to realize that rejection can hurt—especially when we are the one being rejected!

Samuel experienced a sense of rejection when the elders of the nation of Israel came to him and demanded a king in his place (1 Sam. 8:6). They pointed out the fact that he was old and that his sons had not been righteous in their offices as judges. These were justifiable reasons, they felt, to change the status quo and incorporate a new form of leadership.

Samuel was somewhat put out by the attitude the elders displayed. When he sought the Lord in prayer, God answered, "Hearken unto the voice of the people in all that they say unto thee: for they have not rejected thee, but they have rejected me, that I should not reign over them" (v. 7).

God had put His finger on the pulse of the problem, and at the same time, He had reassured his aging prophet: The elders weren't rejecting Samuel's leadership; they were rejecting God.

Even so, whatever the other person's motivation might be, when we are rejected, it can be a devastating thing. My third-grade teacher rejected me because my family was poor, and in her mind, this indicated that I was lazy, worthless and a waste of her time. She was basing her assessment of me on her preconceived notion of what "project people" were all about: crime, immorality and general laziness.

THE CRIPPLING POWER OF REJECTION

Rejection can become a fatal distraction for several reasons. First, it can be emotionally debilitating. Proverbs 18:21 says, "Death and life are in the power of the tongue." My teacher's harsh words nearly killed me emotionally that day, and nothing short of the grace, power and provision of God could have restored a sense of well-being and hope to me again. Maybe a trusted friend, a parent or a husband has rejected you—this can easily strip you of your sense of self-worth and your personal pride.

> Rejection can hurt—especially when you are the one being rejected!

Second, rejection can become a fatal distraction when you take ownership of it, believing yourself to be worthy of the rejection. You may make life choices based on what you have been told about yourself rather than on what God has to say about you. My teacher told me I would never get out of the projects, and I believed her. I accepted her rejection as valid, and from that moment on, I began to look at myself through her eyes instead of God's.

Many women in ministry cope with the pain of rejection on a regular basis. We are often rejected because of the simple reality of our being *female*—and many persons are not accepting of a *woman* who delivers the Word of God. They bluntly state, "I don't believe in women preachers!" Subsequently, they close their ears, their minds and their hearts to anything a woman in ministry has to say. We not only have to cope with our *words* not being received, but the rejection also subjects us to undue and unnecessary spiritual warfare. We war with the spirits of criticism and rejection that come against us, and we war with the painful sting of the rejection that we receive.

What the Bible says is true: "As he thinks within himself, so he is" (Prov. 23:7, NAS). It is imperative that we replace rejection with the life-giving, life-changing Word of God, which assures us in Jeremiah 29:11, "For I know the thoughts that I think toward you, says the LORD, thoughts of peace and not of evil, to give you a future and a hope" (NKJV).

Yes, the words and attitudes of other people can deeply wound us, but they do not have to destroy us. Although we all desire the acceptance and appreciation of others, we must always keep in mind that ultimately, what is most important is how God sees us. We must "let God be true, and every man a liar" when it comes to experiencing rejection. (See Romans 3:4.)

The fatal distraction of rejection can also bring other fatal distractions such as hurt, loneliness, anger and bitterness. Let's face it; rejection hurts, and when we nurse that hurt, it can distract us from God's plan for our lives. Rejection often causes loneliness, for we isolate ourselves and withdraw from others when we believe that we are not "good enough." Hurt and loneliness will lead to anger—not only at the person who rejected us, but also toward ourselves. We begin to wonder, *Why do I have to be this way? Why can't I be more lovable or more attractive?* Finally, we become bitter about our lot in life and feel that we have been dealt an unfair hand. Dealing with just one of these fatal distractions is bad enough, but to have rejection, hurt, loneliness, anger and bitterness at work all at the same time can be almost unbearable!

A WAY OUT

I am so grateful to God that His grace did not permit me to live my entire life under a cloud of rejection. Things began to change when I moved in with Big Mama (my grandmother on my mother's side). Big Mama didn't have any better sense than to believe that, regardless of our poverty and social status, we were the people God said we were, and that was that! Big Mama pumped me full of the Word of God and her affirming love. She constantly told me that I was a child of the King, that I had royal blood flowing through my veins, and that I was going to grow up to be "a mighty woman in the Lord!" The fact that God's Word gave her hope allowed her to instill hope in my life. In hindsight, it amazes me how she was able to fulfill God's directives:

> Therefore shall ye lay up these my words in your heart and in your soul, and bind them for a sign upon your hand, that they may be as frontlets between your eyes. And ye shall teach them [to] your children, speaking of them when thou sittest in thine house, and when

thou walkest by the way, when thou liest down,
and when thou risest up.
—Deuteronomy 11:18–19, emphasis added

Slowly but surely, through her love and by the sheer power of the Word, Big Mama eradicated the fatal distraction of rejection from my life. Oh, how I thank God for that! Against all odds, I went on to become a cheerleader and the homecoming queen, and I was even voted "most popular" in my senior class! I eventually graduated from college and have traveled all over the world. And I am currently enjoying a life enhanced by the blessings, favor and anointing of God.

God doesn't want to bless just me—His deliverance is available for all who will turn to Him. Are you a woman in ministry who is struggling with the reality of rejection? Strive to remain undaunted by it, and focus instead upon the security of your divine calling; refuse to allow rejection to make you bitter and retaliatory.

> Allow the love of God to flow into you, and watch His glory and grace be manifested in your life.

Woman of God, are you plagued by the fatal distraction of rejection? Have you taken ownership of the disparaging things that have been said about you and attributed the rejection of others to be rejection by God as well? By the love of God and the power and authority of His Word, I say to you, "Not so!" God is your Light, your Savior, your Protector and your Shield. His banner over you is love (Song of Sol. 2:4). He loved you before you were even born, so much so that He sent His only Son to die in your place. You are special, you are precious in His sight, and you are important to the kingdom of God! Even if the past things that were said about you were justified, know that your Lord Jesus Christ is able to make all things new. He can and He will erase the ugliness of your past and give you a life that's fresh and clean. Choose this day to say and believe only what God says about you, and allow the Word of God to drive out every contrary thought. Bring your thoughts into captivity of the obedience of Christ, as 2 Corinthians 10:5 tells us. Know above all else that, according to Ephesians 1:6, He has made you accepted in His beloved Son, and that "in every nation whoever fears Him and works righteousness is accepted by Him" (Acts 10:35, NKJV).

God accepts you, and He wants to bring healing and restoration to your damaged emotions. Allow the love of God to flow into you, and watch His glory and grace be manifested in your life. Rise up in the name of Jesus, and be healed in your mind, your body and your spirit!

On the other hand, I admonish each of you to be extremely mindful of the words you speak to others. Ask God to help you deal with your prejudices and preconceived notions about other people, and be especially careful of the liberty you take in expressing your opinions. If you have been blessed with children, do as Big Mama did, and constantly pour the Word of God into them. Let them know that they are loved, not only by God, but also by you, and that they are valuable persons in your life. Help them understand that God has a divine purpose and destiny for their lives and that they are special.

Guard your interactions with all people, no matter

their race, creed or national origin. Keep in mind that all men are made in the image and likeness of God, that He "hath made of one blood all nations of men for to dwell on the face of the earth, and hath determined the times before appointed, and the bounds of their habitation; that they should seek the Lord, if haply they might feel after him, and find him, though he be not far from every one of us" (Acts 17:26–27).

Strive to speak only words that are godly to the use of edifying. Be used by God to verbally pronounce blessings—not by the devil to speak judgments and curses. Remember, the words you speak will make a difference in someone's life—whether for good or for evil—so always ensure that the difference you make is a positive one.

CHAPTER 16

Your Greatest Distraction Is You!

Your Greatest Distraction Is You!

S o many other distractions take our attention away from what God wants for us: busy schedules, "difficult" people, financial problems, the annoying habits of others, the threat of terrorism and war—and let's not forget our personal drama of the week! It all boils down to this disturbing reality: Our most fatal distraction comes from within ourselves.

Pogo, the political cartoon character from the 1950s, stated, "We have met the enemy and it is us!"[1] The apostle Paul expressed the same sentiment in Romans 7:22–25 (TLB):

> I love to do God's will, so far as my new nature is concerned; but there is something else deep within me, in my lower nature, that is at war with my mind and wins the fight and makes me a slave to the sin that is still within me...Who will free me from my slavery to this deadly lower nature? Thank God it has been done by Jesus Christ our Lord.

All of the fatal distractions discussed in this book can destroy you, but only if you allow them to do so. And it may very well be that the only distraction that is holding you back is you!

FATAL DISTRACTIONS

Have you ever heard the expression about a person's being "their own worst enemy"? Well, it's true! Constantly thinking negative thoughts or pursuing self-destructive behaviors and habits can make you your own worst enemy. Focusing on the lives of others rather than developing your own is like sitting in the bleachers instead of getting out on the field with the team—

Fatal distractions can destroy you, but only if you allow them to do so.

and your life will waste away in the process. We shouldn't spend an inordinate amount of time trying to police what others are doing. If all I do is look at you and try to keep tabs on the affairs of your life, one of two things will happen: I will either start trying to outdo you, or I'll begin to think I'm superior to you. Paul made this indictment about people who focused too much on what other people were doing:

> For we are not bold to class or compare ourselves with some of those who commend themselves; but when they measure themselves by themselves, and compare themselves with themselves, they are without understanding.
> —2 CORINTHIANS 10:12, NAS

Paul certainly seemed to understand human nature, didn't he? He was saying that when we compare ourselves with others and think we're better than they are, we are "without understanding"—in other words, we are *dumb!*

Not only do we need to get over *other people,* but we also need to get over *ourselves!* We need to stop worrying about others and get a life! It is entirely up to us to *choose* life. God made this clear in Deuteronomy 30:15, 19:

> See, I have set before thee this day life and good, and death and evil . . . I call heaven and earth to record this day against you, that I have set before you life and death, blessing and cursing: therefore choose life, that both thou and thy seed may live.

Don't you like how God gives us the right answers? In case you didn't know which choice to make, He tells you: *Choose life!* The word *choose* means that we have a decision to make; the ball is in our court. Big Mama would often say that we won't get to heaven by accident—we have to *purpose* to live right so we can get there. We all need to get a life—but *we can choose the life we get.* Sometimes we have to go through a number of hardships before we understand what this really means.

THE SPIRITUAL SCHOOL OF OBEDIENCE

When many people buy a puppy, they sometimes send it to obedience school so it can learn how to obey its new master. In much the same way, God sends *us* to His "school of obedience"! In Hebrews 5:7–9, we see that Jesus Himself learned about obedience in this school:

> Who in the days of his flesh, when he had offered up prayers and supplications with strong crying and tears unto him that was able to save him from death, and was heard in that he feared; though he were a Son, yet learned he obedience by the things which he suffered; and being made perfect, he became the author of eternal salvation unto all them that obey him.

Even though we all understand what a "school" is, we may have more trouble with the definition of *obedience*. *Obedience* is "an act or instance of obeying." To *obey* means to "follow the commands or guidance of; to conform to or comply with; to behave obediently."[2] The school where we learn obedience isn't a "natural" school, like obedience school for puppies, or even our own high schools or universities. It is a *spiritual* school, not made with human hands—its Builder and Maker is God. He determines when you go to this school, and He alone determines what classes you take when He sends you there. This is the school where the "diploma" you get is a real testimony, and the "degree" you earn is an in-depth experience with God!

In the school of obedience, God "prunes your branches"—you learn to put away *your* own mind-set, *your* own ideas, *your* own way; it is where you learn to truthfully say, "Lord, what would *You* have me to do?"

When we are going through the school of obedience, we can look to the promise contained in Jeremiah 33:3, which says, "Call unto me, and I will answer thee, and shew thee great and might things, which thou knowest not." We are told in Psalm 91:15, "He shall call upon me, and I will answer him: I will be with him in trouble; I will deliver him, and honour him."

Paul wrote in seven different passages, "Brethren, I would not have you be ignorant..." In other words, God wants you to be aware of what is going on! Not only do you have a *need* for instruction, but also God is ready, willing and able to give it to you.

How many of us have missed—or almost missed—

healings, deliverances and blessings because we had set our minds on their coming a *certain way?* The simple fact that we *need* instruction from God ought to let us know that we are in no position to expect or demand it to come a certain way.

When you say you want God to speak to you, He will! But if you demand that He speak a certain way—*your* way—you won't hear what He has to say. He may be speaking to you through your pastor on Sunday morning or when you're at Bible study on Wednesday night. God may speak to you through a conference

> When you first deal with the internal problem of yourself, your other problems will then be easier to untangle.

speaker, or He may do it through your teenage son or daughter. He may even speak to you through the lives and examples of fellow believers.

If you are going to learn to deal effectively with the internal distraction of yourself, you are going to have to pass through this school of obedience. No matter how serious your problems might be, the ultimate solution lies in the way *you* handle them. When you first deal with the internal problem of *yourself,* your other problems will then be easier to untangle.

DEALING WITH THE INNER PROBLEM OF "YOU"

There are ways that we deal with problems that not only prevent us from *solving* the problem, but also actually make matters worse! When Jesus was confronted in the Garden of Gethsemane, Peter responded in an inappropriate way by using his sword to cut off a soldier's ear (Matt. 26:51)! This could have destroyed *him* if the soldiers had decided to attack. Jesus told Peter, "Put up again thy sword into his place: for all they that take the sword shall perish with the sword" (v. 52). Peter did not know how to solve his problem, and he dealt with it the only way he knew how—in the flesh.

God's divine metamorphosis changes us and drives out the undesirable elements of our personalities.

One of the reasons Peter was not equipped to deal with the problem was that he had not yet received the baptism of the Holy Spirit, and he resorted to using a physical, carnal weapon against the opposition that Jesus was facing. Many of us today have an advantage in that we have received the baptism of the Holy Spirit, but if we do not remain controlled by the Spirit, we will resort to using carnal weapons as well. Second Corinthians 10:3–4 declares:

> For though we walk in the flesh, we do not war after the flesh: (For the weapons of our warfare are not carnal, but mighty through God to the pulling down of strong holds).

THE DIVINE METAMORPHOSIS

Whatever problems you are facing, you can rejoice, because the weapons of your warfare are mighty. And when you learn to put aside the internal distraction of *you*,

you can use those weapons more effectively for the kingdom of God. Begin to grow in the knowledge of God and who you are in Him. Like the caterpillar that goes into the cocoon and emerges as a beautiful butterfly, let God work a "divine metamorphosis" in you. When this divine metamorphosis takes place inside you, you no longer are an internal distraction to yourself, and the attributes that God desires to manifest in your life will come to fruition.

How can this metamorphosis take place in our lives today? It happens as we behold the glory of the Lord! Consider the words of 2 Corinthians 3:18: "But we all, with open face beholding as in a glass the glory of the Lord, are changed into the same image from glory to glory, even as by the Spirit of the Lord."

God's divine metamorphosis changes us and drives out the undesirable elements of our personalities, replacing them with the things of God. We are being transformed *into His image*. God created man in His image, as we read in Genesis 1:27, but that original image was marred when sin entered the world.

No one can spend *quality* time in the presence of God and not be *changed*. We can't experience a genuine time of fellowship in His presence, and then immediately turn around and backbite one another, lying or speaking harsh, ungodly words to one another. James 3:10–12 addresses this disparity in speech:

> Out of the same mouth proceedeth blessing and cursing. My brethren, these things ought not so to be. Doth a fountain send forth at the same place sweet water and bitter? Can the fig tree, my brethren, bear olive berries? Either a

vine, figs? So can no fountain both yield salt
water and fresh.

Our time with Him will be reflected in our being more
like Him.

When we experience a divine metamorphosis, we will
experience *change* on the inside. Changing externally is
like rearranging furniture in a room—you may get new
drapes or change the color of the carpet, but guess what?
It's still the same room! Make sure your personal metamorphosis is *internal,* where it really matters, where it really
counts.

Look at the internal distraction that is *yourself* realis-
tically, and don't sugarcoat anything the Holy Spirit
reveals to you. Let this be a defining moment in your life—
that moment in time when something profound, earth-
shattering or even life-changing occurs. You will never be
the same again.

CONCLUSION

Women's Vital Role in the Kingdom

W E ARE LIVING in the last days of God's timetable for the world, but we are also living in the one-minute-to-midnight timeframe of our individual lives. We have no time to waste on any distraction, fatal or otherwise. Women have too vital a part to play in the plan of salvation. Women have too great a part to play in the deliverance of their families. Women have too vital a role to play in ministry to other women and to the entire body of Christ. The apostle Peter proclaimed on the Day of Pentecost, "But this is that which was spoken by the prophet Joel; and it shall come to pass in the last days, saith God, I will pour out of my Spirit upon all flesh: and your sons and *your daughters* shall prophesy" (Acts 2:16–17, emphasis added). Women can't afford to be delayed, detoured or distracted from their destinies! Even a short delay can be fatal to those following us, as well as to the generations at risk who will be impacted by our ministries.

The world declares, "Knowledge is power." That is true in the spiritual realm as well. The devil wants to keep his subtle devices hidden. Nevertheless, the apostle Paul wrote, "We are not ignorant of his [Satan's] devices" (2 Cor. 2:11).

FATAL DISTRACTIONS

Sometimes these devices are *external* to us, but these are not usually fatal to us. It is not our failing marriages or the heartbreak over being unequally yoked that will deter us from our destiny. It is not being unloved, as Leah was. It is not being in an abusive relationship, as Abigail was. It is not our work, our health or our commitment to senior parents that can stress us to the point of missing God and His purpose for our lives. No, the distractions that truly circumvent our futures only come from within. They can only come from *ourselves*.

Women can't afford to be delayed, detoured or distracted from their destinies!

If you are facing a fatal internal distraction, take this moment while the waters of your spirit are troubled, and come before God, praying the following prayer:

> *Father, in Jesus' name, I confess my distractions now to You. I release them, knowing that I can cast my cares upon You because You care for me. I believe that whatever I place into Your capable hands is dissolved forever from mine. Lord, cancel the power of these distractions over me, never allowing them to hinder me again. I speak to any external distraction in my life: my job, a toxic relationship, health issues, substance abuse problems, financial distress, past childhood experiences, family dysfunction or even ancestral and generational curses. By the authority of Your Word and because You love me unconditionally, I*

declare that I am an overcomer! Lord, I renounce my own ways and surrender to Your way for me. I joyfully and with anticipation begin the journey to my destiny with You, knowing that the safest place for me is in Your chosen path for my life.

God, I now take the courage to deal with my internal distractions. I call my distractions what they are. I look at myself truthfully and confess that I have been my own "fatal distraction." I see the flaws that could have been fatal, but Your grace and mercy have given me this opportunity to be healed. I call out the names of my internal distractions: selfishness and her sisters, envy and jealousy; loneliness and isolation; anger; bitterness; hurt; fear; rejection; and even myself.

I have confidence that as I release these negative distractions from my life, You will align my life and future into the "expected end" you have promised for me in Jeremiah 29:11.

Lord, thank You for doing a new thing in me. Thank You for proving Your love for me yet again. Thank You for putting me again on Your track for my destiny. Thank You for restoration, purpose and healing.

In Jesus' name I pray all of these things. Amen.

Now that every distraction has been canceled by the power of the Holy Spirit, I declare healing and wholeness to your life. You *will* be a person of purpose. You *will* retain your godly focus. You *will* operate in the gifts and callings the Lord has placed on your life. The Spirit of God will stir up the gifts that He has placed in you, and you will go forth in a great army of women doing God's will and God's work for the kingdom.

Make the following confession, and become a part of what God is doing through women on the earth.

> I will not be distracted anymore. I will not look to the left or the right. I will look only to Jesus who is the Author and Finisher of my faith. My eyes are on the cross. My eyes are on the prize of the high calling of God, which is in Christ Jesus. I see myself in a glorious future, full of purpose and power. I have been fearfully and wonderfully made, and I am all that I am called to be in God. I am powerful. I am a warrior for His purpose. I am a mender of the breach.
>
> I am an ambassador for Christ. I am a woman of destiny, and I will not be distracted anymore!

Notes

INTRODUCTION
FATAL DISTRACTIONS

1. *Merriam-Webster's Collegiate Dictionary*, tenth edition (Springfield, MA: Merriam-Webster, Inc., 1995), s.v. "wiles."
2. "For the Media: Women's Health Statistical Information: Leading Causes of Death for American Women by Racial/Ethnic Group (2000)," The National Women's Health Information Center, 4woman.gov. Retrieved from the Internet on July 3, 2003 at www.4woman.gov/media/chart.htm. Also, "For the Media: Women's Health Statistical Information," The National Women's Health Information Center, 4woman.gov. Retrieved from the Internet on July 3, 2003 at www.4woman.gov/media/statinfo.htm.

CHAPTER 1
ONE MINUTE BEFORE MIDNIGHT

1. *Merriam-Webster's Collegiate Dictionary*, s.v. "fatal."
2. Ibid., "distract."
3. Ibid.

CHAPTER 2
DYSFUNCTIONAL FAMILY PATTERNS:
THE HERITAGE OF LEAH

1. Nelson's Bible Dictionary, PC Study Bible for Windows, version 1.4, copyright © 1993, 1994, Biblesoft, s.v. "Reuben."
2. Ibid., s.v. "Simeon."
3. Ibid., s.v. "Levi."
4. Ibid., s.v. "Judah."

CHAPTER 3
JOB CONCERNS: THE "MARTHA SYNDROME"

1. Tracee Cornforth, "Stress and Your Health." Retrieved

from the Internet July 8, 2003 at http://womenshealth. about.com/library/weekly/aa051799.htm.

CHAPTER 6
MARITAL PROBLEMS:
THE POSITIVE ATTITUDE OF ABIGAIL

1. *Oxford English Dictionary*, unabridged edition (New York: Oxford University Press), s.v. "nabal."

CHAPTER 9
ENVY AND JEALOUSY

1. *Merriam-Webster's Collegiate Dictionary*, s.v. "jealousy."
2. Ibid.
3. Ibid., s.v. "envy."

CHAPTER 10
LONELINESS

1. *Merriam-Webster's Collegiate Dictionary*, s.v. "alone."
2. Ibid., s.v. "loneliness."

CHAPTER 11
ANGER

1. *Merriam-Webster's Collegiate Dictionary*, s.v. "anger."
2. Ibid., s.v. "antagonism."
3. Ibid., s.v. "anger."
4. Ibid., s.v. "wrath."

CHAPTER 12
BITTERNESS

1. *Merriam-Webster's Collegiate Dictionary*, s.v. "bitter."
2. Ibid., s.v. "bitterness."

CHAPTER 13
HURT AND BROKENNESS

1. *Merriam-Webster's Collegiate Dictionary*, s.v. "hurt."
2. Ibid.

3. Ibid., s.v. "broken."
4. Ibid., s.v. "pain."
5. "It Is Well With My Soul" by Horatio G. Spafford. Public domain.
6. *Merriam-Webster's Collegiate Dictionary*, s.v. "pain."

CHAPTER 14
FEAR

1. *Merriam-Webster's Collegiate Dictionary*, s.v. "fear."
2. Ibid., s.v. "afraid."

CHAPTER 15
REJECTION

1. *Merriam-Webster's Collegiate Dictionary*, s.v. "rejection."

CHAPTER 16
YOUR GREATEST DISTRACTION IS YOU!

1. Walt Kelly, creator of Pogo, "Quote Me On It . . ." Retrieved from the Internet on July 18, 2003 at www.quotemeonit.com/enemy.html.
2. *Merriam-Webster's Collegiate Dictionary*, s.v. "obey;" "obedience."

Primary Purpose Ministries Recommends Other Powerful Resources

11:59: "A Time of Transition"

God's promises and prophetic utterances for our lives always proceed the manifestation of His Word. It's 11:59, the waiting period between God's promise and the fulfillment of the promise. What do you do while you are waiting? Available on CD and audiocassette.

This Is Only a Test

If you are experiencing jarring, piercing and unbearable circumstances in your life, Evangelist Rodgers encourages you to stand still; "this is only a test." Available on audiocassette and videocassette.

The Three Dimensions of Yes

Join Evangelist Rodgers on a journey into the three dimensions of "yes": "yes" in your mind, "yes" in your will and "yes" in your spirit. Available on audiocassette and videocassette.

I Won't Leave Until...

Have you ever been tempted to give up, quit and throw in the towel? This message explores the Jacob-like vigor of spiritually wrestling to obtain a blessing from the Lord without giving up, leaving or letting go. Available on audiocassette and videocassette.

Get Out of the Boat

How often are you provoked to press beyond your flesh, obstacles and even people to do the miraculous? Get out of the boat! You can walk on water. Available on audiocassette and videocassette.

Incredible Praise for Incredible Blessings

Psalm 149 encourages us to praise the Lord! It means to literally make a fool out of yourself for the Lord. Offering incredible praise unto the Lord will cause inconceivable blessings to manifest. Available on audiocassette and videocassette.

The Fight Is Fixed

Generally, when you hear, "The fight is fixed," you think, *How unfair!* or *They didn't even stand a chance.* In this case, the fight has been fixed or prearranged in your favor! Available on audiocassette and videocassette.

Embrace Your Miracle

In certain seasons of life, it may appear that "the promise" has died. You've just entered a new season, and it's your time to embrace your miracle. Go ahead! Available on audiocassette and videocassette.

Deliverance NOW

Snap! This is the sound of deliverance. Hear the prophetic instructions from God as you experience deliverance *now*. Available on audiocassette and videocassette.

To order or for more information, contact:

Primary Purpose Ministries
c/o Joyce L. Rodgers
608 Lakey Street
Denton, Texas 76205
Phone: (940) 323-0754
Website: www.Primary-Purpose.org